Learn Chinese Through 100 Sentence Frames

100句式汉语通

鲁 川　孙文访 ◎ 著

华语教学出版社
SINOLINGUA

First Edition 2011

ISBN 978-7-5138-0036-5

Copyright 2011 by Sinolingua

Published by Sinolingua

24 Baiwanzhuang Road, Beijing 100037, China

Tel: (86) 10-68320585 68997826

Fax: (86) 10-68997826 68326333

http://www.sinolingua.com.cn

E-mail: hyjx@sinolingua.com.cn

Printed by Beijing Mixing Printing Co., Ltd.

Printed in the People's Republic of China

1. Readers

Learn Chinese Through 100 Sentence Frames is for English speakers in the global community who are interested in China or visiting China. The readers' knowledge of Chinese can be very basic or even nonexistent, and they can use this book to teach themselves Chinese in their own time and at their own pace.

2. Contents

The number of practical sentences in a language is infinite, but the number of sentence models is finite. The sentence models of syntactic structure are called sentence patterns, they number less than 10 and are comprised of the syntactic constituents of a sentence such as the subject, predicate, object, attribute, adverbial, and complement. In this book, the sentence models of semantic meaning, called sentence frames, have been adopted as a teaching tool.

There are around 100 sentence frames, which are classified by semantic categories including time, location, source, goals, etc. A more detailed explanation of the classification can be found in one of the following sections, "Semantic Categories in Sentence Frames".

This book is organized into ten chapters, each addressing a different topic area that will provide the readers with knowledge that they will frequently find useful when traveling and living in China. Each topic area includes ten practical sentence frames which reflect the types of daily situations that the readers may encounter, with the book providing a total of 100 situational sentence frames. As well as these frames, other related practical vocabulary is also provided for each situation, allowing the readers to conveniently substitute related vocabulary into the sentence frames and create new sentences for their specific needs.

The ten topic areas are as follows:

I. Useful Expressions	II. Persons and Things	III. Time and Location	IV. Shopping
V. Eating and Drinking	VI. Accommodation	VII. Transportation	
VIII. Studying and Working	IX. Culture and Recreation		
X. Sports and Health			

3. How to use this book?

This book is different from Chinese textbooks used in the classroom. We have made the needs of beginners our first priority and put emphasis on training the readers to teach themselves to the best of their abilities.

(1) The readers will first learn a few useful phrases, such as standard greetings and introductions; expressions of happiness and praise; making apologies; saying goodbye, etc.

(2) They will then be able to search for more specific English sentence frames, based on their needs, in the contents section. For example, if a reader wants to say, "Where is the subway station?" they should first locate VII. Transportation 交通 [jiāotōng] and there they will find sentence frame 068:

068 Where is the subway station?

地铁站在哪里？　　　　　　　Dìtiězhàn zài nǎli？

(3) The ability to ask questions under many different conditions will be looked at especially. The first sentence of the title of each sentence frame is interrogative, and related to the declarative sentence in the frame. If the readers master the usage of interrogative sentences, they will be able to use their Chinese to ask for any information they may need, and as they enlarge their Chinese vocabulary they will be able to create more and

more such sentences.

(4) In this book, each sentence frame is comprised of a table of columns, one for each semantic category. The first line of the table shows the sequence positions, which never number more than nine.

(5) In this book, each sentence frame page contains a sentence frame table, a vocabulary table, and grammar notes. Students teaching themselves are recommended to concentrate on the sentence frames table, for the Chinese language doesn't have morphological changes. The main grammatical means of Chinese is word order, and sentence frames provide learners with both the sequences of categories in basic Chinese sentences and their equivalent sequences in English sentences. The vocabulary table words are optional, and can be learned by the readers at their leisure, according to their individual needs.

(6) Generally speaking, without context displacement, the order of the meaning categories in Chinese basic sentence frames is fixed. This order is as follows: ① subjective; ② causative; ③ time; ④ location; ⑤ follower; ⑥ beneficiary; ⑦ verbal ⑧ dative; ⑨ objective.

The predicate verb of a sentence will occur in the sequence position of number seven ⑦. This verb mainly gives expression to actions, states, mentalities, possessions etc.

4. The main features of Chinese grammar explained in the notes

In this book, the features of Chinese grammar are explained in the grammar notes of the sentence frames. They are briefly as follows:

(1) In Chinese, words don't have morphological changes. For example, Chinese verbs don't have tenses and voices, and adjectives need not be changed into comparative degrees, such as "good → better → best" in comparative sentences.

(2) The word order of interrogative sentences is the same as that of declarative sentences.

① "吗 [ma]" is positioned at the end of a declarative sentence to form a yes-or-no question.

② To form interrogative sentences, interrogative pronouns (Wh-) are positioned in sentences where the answers are expected to occur.

(3) The attributes and attributive clauses are always positioned before the head.

(4) The adverbials and adverbial clauses are always positioned before the predicate verb in a sentence.

(5) The complement indicates the result, direction and degree of an action, state or change; therefore, it always follows directly after the predicate verb in a sentence.

(6) The basic structural unit of Chinese is a monosyllabic sinogram. In general, one sinogram represents one basic concept, and combinations of two or more sinograms denote compound concepts.

(7) The main type of word formation of Chinese compound nouns is "attribute + head." In general, the attributes are sinograms that indicate the features of the heads, and the heads are sinograms that represent categories. In the following words: "卧室 [wòshì] (bedroom)", "教室 [jiàoshì] (classroom)", "暗室 [ànshì] (darkroom)", "展室 [zhǎnshì] (showroom)", "调度室 [diàodùshì] (control room)", "阅览室 [yuèlǎnshì] (reading room)", "吸烟室 [xīyānshì] (smoking room)", "会议室 [huìyìshì] (meeting room)", the sinogram "室 [shì]" represents the "room" category.

5. Marks

[　] contains the Pinyin of Chinese words, for example, in "爸 [bà]."

(　) contains the English or Chinese translation, for example, in "爸 (dad)."

{　} contains material that may be omitted.

一、《100 句式汉语通》的对象

《100 句式汉语通》面向全世界对中国感兴趣或来中国观光的外国人。读者可以是汉语水平为"零"或具有初级汉语水平的自学者，但他们都应以英语为母语或第二语言。

二、《100 句式汉语通》的内容

一种语言的"实际句子"是无限的,而"句子模式"是有限的。句法上的句子模式叫做"句型",以"主语、谓语、宾语、状语、补语"的句子成分来展示。"句型"种类太少而不到 10 个。本书采用语义上的 100 种句子模式,叫做"句式",以"时间、地点、起点、终点"的语义类别 (义类) 来展示。(详见后面的"句式中的义类")。

本书提供 : ①英汉对照的"句式框架",②英汉对照的"分类词语",③英汉对照的"语法注解",④英汉对照的"情景对话";也就是"句式框架、填充词语、语法要点、情景交际"的四结合。本书按"情景"分为 10 大部分。每个部分包括 10 个"句式框架",共计"100 个适应情景的句式框架"(详见后面"句式的目录")。

三、《100 句式汉语通》的编写方式和学习者如何使用这本书

本书跟其他在课堂学习汉语的课本不同。编写时首先考虑的是初学汉语者的需求和对其自学能力的培养。

1. 先学一些最有用的交际"短句",如 : "打招呼,表示高兴,相互介绍,称赞,感谢,道歉,再见"等等。

2. 学习者根据自己想说的内容,从目录的"情景"中找到所需的英语句式。如想说"Where is the subway station?"在目录中找到"VII. Transportation 交通",就能找到所需的 068 句式 : "Where is the subway station? 地铁站在哪里？"

3. 尽快培养学习者独立获取汉语知识的自学能力,特别是在各种条件下如何"提问题"的询问能力。每个句式框架的标题中的第一行句子都是一个向框架中的"叙述句"提问的"疑问句"。学习者学会了"疑问句"就能在各种"情景"中向当地人询问和请教,随时随地扩充自己的汉语词汇和句子。

4. 一个"句式"是由若干个"义类栏"所组成的"表格"。表格的第一行是"序位",序位最多不超过 9 个。

5. 每一个"句式"占一页,上半页是句式"表格",下半页是"词语"表,中间是"注解"即语法提示。对于自学者来说,上半页的"句式"是要掌握的重点,因为汉语没有"词形变化",最主要的语法手段就是"语序"。着重地掌握上半页的"句式"就是尽快学会汉语常用句的"语序"。至于下半页的"词语"表是自由掌握的,即根据自己的条件逐步学习的,即使暂时不学下半页的"词语"表也不妨碍学习下一个上半页的"句式"。

6. 汉语基本句式各种"义类"的顺序是固定的,在没有"语境移位"的条件下,基本句式的"义类"顺序如下 : ①主体,②原由,③时间,④地点,⑤伴体,⑥涉体,⑦述谓,⑧邻体,⑨客体。

其中第⑦序位"述谓"就是句子的谓语动词,主要体现为"动作、状态、存在、心态、领有、联系"等。

四、《100 句式汉语通》的"注解"中叙述了汉语语法的主要特点

本书的"注解"针对各个"句式"的内容,分散地叙述了汉语语法的特点。归纳起来主要有下列几点:

1. 汉语没有"词形变化",动词没有"时态、语态"的变化,形容词没有"级"的变化等。

2. 汉语"疑问句"的语序跟"叙述句"的语序基本相同:

　　①"是否疑问句"在"叙述句"之后加"吗"。

　　②"特指疑问句"中的"疑问词"的位置就是它所指代的"词语"在叙述句中原来的位置。

3. 汉语"定语"一律在"中心语"之前。

4. 汉语"状语"一律在"谓语动词"之前。

5. 汉语"补语"表示"行动"的结局、趋向或程度。一律在"谓语动词"之后。

6. 汉语的基本结构单位是单音节的"字",通常一个"字"表示一个简单概念。几个"字"组合表示复合概念。

7. 汉语构词类型最多的是"定中结构",其中前边是"特征字",后边是"类别字"。汉语"类别字"之一相当于英语的 -room (室)。例如:"卧室" (bedroom)、"教室" (classroom)、"暗室" (darkroom)、"展室" (showroom)、"调度室" (control room)、"阅览室" (reading room)、"吸烟室" (smoking room)、"会议室" (meeting room)。

五、《100 句式汉语通》所用符号的说明

　　[ ] 内为汉语词语的"拼音",如:"爸 [bà]"。(　　) 内为英语或汉语对译。{ 　　 } 表示省略。

Introduction to *Pinyin* of Chinese 汉语"拼音"简介

The script of Chinese is sinograms (Chinese characters). Each sinogram has a distinct pronunciation. *Pinyin* is a set of phonetic symbols used for noting the pronunciation of sinograms. In this book, the pinyin for words can be found in this notation [ ], such as in 爸 [bà](dad).

汉语的文字是"汉字"(曾译为 Chinese characters 现根据《文字学术语》译为 sinograms)。每个汉字都有确定的读音。"拼音"是标注汉字读音的符号,本书中汉语词汇的"拼音"置于 [ ] 内,如:爸 [bà] (dad)。

1. Chinese syllables 汉语的音节。

The pronunciation of a sinogram is a *syllable*, which consists of three parts: ① an *initial* (the beginning consonant), ② a *final* (the rear vowels and nasal consonants), ③ and a *tone* (the rise and fall of sound within the whole syllable). For instance, in the syllable "爸 [bà]", "b" is the initial, "a" is the final, " ` " over the final vowel is the tone.

The *tone* is not only the rise and fall sound in the *final*, but the rise and fall of sound in the whole syllable, as follows.

a syllable (音节) : bà [爸] (dad)	(the tone) `	
	(the initial) b	a (the final)

一个汉字的读音是一个"音节"。音节由三个部分组成:①声母(音节开头的辅音)、②韵母(音节后部的元音及鼻辅音)、③声调(整个音节的升和降)。如"爸 [bà]":"b"是声母,"a"是韵母,上方的" ` "是声调。声调不只是"韵母"的升和降,而是包括"声母"和"韵母"的整个"音节"的升和降,如上图所示。

2. The following are the *initials* and their similar English phonemes. 下面是"声母"及近似的英语发音。

Initial 声母	Similar English 近似音	Initial 声母	Similar English 近似音	Initial 声母	Similar English 近似音
b	like "b" in "boob"	g	like "g" in "get"	sh	like "sh" in "shoot"
p	like "p" in "poop"	k	like "k" in "kept"	r	like "r" in "root"
m	like "m" in "mood"	h	like "h" in "hat"	z	like "ds" in "goods"
f	like "f" in "food"	j	like "j" in "jeep"	c	like "ts" in "boots"
d	like "d" in "dab"	q	like "ch" in "cheep"	s	like "s" in "bus"
t	like "t" in "tab"	x	like "sh" in "sheep"	w	like "w" in "wet"
n	like "n" in "nab"	zh	like "dr" in "droop"	y	like "y" in "yet"
l	like "l" in "lab"	ch	like "tr" in "troop"		

3. The following are the *finals* and their similar English phonemes. 下面是"韵母"及近似的英语发音。

Final 韵母	Similar English 近似音	Final 韵母	Similar English 近似音	Final 韵母	Similar English 近似音
a	like "a" in "father"	o	like "or" in "order" (英 Br.)	in	like "in" in "machine"
e	like "er" in "her" (英 Br.)	ao	like "ow" in "now"	un	like "oon" in "moon"
er	like "er" in "her" (美 Am.)	ou	like "ow" in "know"	ün	like "un" in "lune" (法 Fr.)
ie	like "ye" in "yes"	u	like "u" in "blue"	ang	like "ang" in "tang"
i	like "i" in "poise"	iu	like "you" in "youth"	eng	like "ung" in "lung"
ai	like "ai" in "aisle"	ü	like "u" in "lune" (法 Fr.)	ing	like "ing" in "king"
ei	like "ei" in "eight"	an	like "an" in "answer"	ong	like "woo" + "ng"
ui	like "ui" in "fluid"	en	like "earn" in "learn" (英 Br.)	ye	like "ye" in "yet"

① There are other compound finals beginning with " i " and " u ", such as "uang=u+ang". The following are the compound finals.

有些以 "i" 和 "u" 开头的加合韵母："uang=u+ang"，如下表所示。

ia=i+a		iao=i+ao		ian=i+an	iang=i+ang	iong=i+ong
ua=u+a	uo=u+o		uai=u+ai	uan=u+an	uang=u+ang	

② When "u" follows "j, q, x," or "y", it becomes "ü". The pronunciation of "ju" is "jü"; the pronunciation of "yu" is "yü", as follows.

在 "j、q、x、y" 之后，"u=ü"。"ju" 的发音是 "jü"；"yu" 的发音是 "yü"，如下表所示。

ju=jü	jue=jüe	juan=jüan	jun=jün	qu=qü	que=qüe	quan=qüan	qun=qün
xu=xü	xue=xüe	xuan=xüan	xun=xün	yu=yü	yue=yüe	yuan=yüan	yun=yün

4. The following are the *tones* in pinyin. 下面是 "拼音" 的 "声调"。

Tone　声调	Tone mark　调标	Examples　例字
The 1st Tone　第一声	—	八 [bā] eight
The 2nd Tone　第二声	／	拔 [bá] to pull up
The 3rd Tone　第三声	∨	靶 [bǎ] target
The 4th Tone　第四声	＼	爸 [bà] dad
Neutral Tone　轻　声	without tone mark　无调标	吧 [ba] (*part.*)

Semantic Categories in Sentence Frames 句式中的 "义类"

A sentence frame is a table comprised of a number of columns, one for each semantic categories. The semantic categories are the classifications of semantic relationships. The main semantic categories are given below:

一个句式是由若干个 "义类栏" 所组成的表格。"义类" 是按语义关系划分的类。主要的 "义类" 如下：

Subjective 主体	Causative 原由	Time 时间	Location 地点	Follower 伴体	Beneficiary 涉体	Verbal 述谓	Dative 邻体	Objective 客体
Person 人	Reason 理由	Period 时期	Scope 范围	Tool 工具	Substance 实体	Action 行动	Duration 时量	Relative 系体
Determiner 限定	Purpose 目的		Source 起点	Manner 方式		State 状态	Frequency 频量	Belongings 属物
Attribute 属性	Basis 依据		Goal 终点	Material 材料		Linking 联系	Amount 数量	

Some of the meaning categories, such as time, location, source, goal, scope, manner, tool, material, amount, determiner and belongings, are easy to understand and needn't be explained. However, the other terms, such as subjective, objective, dative, beneficiary, follower and relative, can be more difficult to understand. Therefore they are explained below.

有些 "义类" 的术语，如 "时间、地点、起点、终点、范围、方式、工具、材料、数量、限定、属物" 等，是容易理解的，不需再加解释。但是有些 "义类" 的术语，如 "主体、客体、邻体、涉体、伴体、系体" 等，是难以理解的，所以需要进行如下的解释。

(1) *Subjective* is the first substance in an event, including: ① the doer of an action; ② the experiencer of a state, attribute or a change; ③ the initial item of a judgment.

"主体" 是一个事件中的第一 "实体"：① 行动的执行者；② 状态、属性或变化的担当者；③ 判断的首项。

(2) *Objective* is the second substance in an event, including: ① the substance being affected by an action; ② the substance being perceived; ③ the product being made ; ④ the content of information transmitted.

"客体" 是一个事件中的第二 "实体"：① 行动的受者；② 感知的对象；③ 制作的成品；④ 传递的信息内容。

(3) *Dative* is the third substance in an event, including: ① the receiver of a present; ② the receiver of information transmitted.

"邻体" 是一个事件中的第三 "实体"：① 赠送的接受者；② 信息传递的接受者。

(4) *Beneficiary* is another substance in an event, including: ① the substance being benefited; ② the substance suffering loss.

"涉体" 是一个事件中另外的 "实体"：① 受益者；② 受损者。

(5) *Follower* is the substance accompanying the subjective in an event, including: ① the companion of the subjective; ② the substance compared with the subjective in the event.

"伴体" 是一个事件中 "主体" 的伴随者：① 主体的伴侣；② 跟主体相比较的实体。

(6) *Relative* is the substance related with the subjective in an event, including: ① the substance being related to the subjective; ② the final item of a judgment.

"系体" 是一个事件中跟主体有关系的 "实体"：① 主体的关系者；② 判断的末项。

Contents of Sentence Frames 句式的目录

I

Useful Expressions
常用语句 [Chángyòng yǔjù]

001. Hello! 您好！

002. Nice to meet you. 认识你很高兴。

003. No problem. 没问题。

004. Don't worry! 别担心！

005. Happy birthday! 祝你生日快乐！

006. Goodbye! 再见！

007. How are you? 您好吗？　　　　　　　　Fine, and you? 很好，您呢？

008. May I come in? 我可以进来吗？　　　　Come in, please! 请进！

009. I'd better go. 我该走了。　　　　　　Won't you stay a little longer? 再坐一会儿吧！

010. You are really terrific! 你真了不起！　　You are overpraising me. 您过奖了。

Hello!	
你好！	Nǐ hǎo!
Hello!	
您好！	Nín hǎo!
Good morning!	
早上好！	Zǎoshang hǎo!
Good afternoon!	
下午好！	Xiàwǔ hǎo!
Good evening!	
晚上好！	Wǎnshang hǎo!

Notes　注解

1. "你 (you)" is used among peers. "您 (you)" is used to show respect for elder people or those of higher status.
2. In this book the Chinese monosyllabic word "字 (script)" is translated as "sinogram" instead of "Chinese character". The meanings of a sinogram (monosyllabic word) are many, but the meaning of a disyllabic word is more defined. Therefore, in the spoken Chinese language, disyllabic words are more frequently used than monosyllabic words.
1. "你"用于身份同等的人及平辈或晚辈的亲友。"您"用来对长辈或老者及地位较高的人表示尊敬。
2. 本书把汉语对应于单音节的"字 (script)"译为"sinogram"以取代"Chinese character"。一个"字 (sinogram)"的意义较多，而"双音节词"的意义比较明确。在汉语的口语中多用双音节词。

Vocabulary　词语

你 [nǐ]	you	午 [wǔ]	noon
您 [nín]	you (with respect)	上午 [shàngwǔ]	morning; before noon
好 [hǎo]	good; nice; all right	下午 [xiàwǔ]	afternoon
早 [zǎo]	morning; early	中 [zhōng]	middle; mid; center
早上 [zǎoshang]	morning	中午 [zhōngwǔ]	noon; midday
上 [shàng]	up; before; last (week); on	晚 [wǎn]	evening; night; late
下 [xià]	down; after; next; below	晚上 [wǎnshang]	evening

Nice to meet you.

认识你很高兴。Rènshi nǐ hěn gāoxìng.

Nice to meet you.
认识你很高兴。

Rènshi nǐ hěn gāoxìng.

Sit down, please!
请坐!

Qǐng zuò!

Let me introduce you to each other.
我来介绍一下。

Wǒ lái jièshào yíxià.

This is Mr. Li.
这是李先生。

Zhè shì Lǐ xiānsheng.

This is Miss Liu.
这是刘小姐。

Zhè shì Liú xiǎojiě.

Notes 注解

1. Chinese "一下 (once)" is used after verbs, indicating that the action will be of short duration or tentative.
2. When addressing a person in Chinese, the family name of the person is put before his/her title, the order is opposite to that of the English expression. For example, "李先生" is called "Mr. Li（李）" in English, and "刘小姐" is called "Miss Liu（刘）" in English as well.
1. 汉语"一下"用在动词后边，表示做一次短暂的动作或尝试性的动作。
2. 中国人的称呼："姓"在前，"称谓"在后，跟英语称呼的顺序相反。例如："李先生"，"刘小姐"。

Vocabulary 词语

很 [hěn]	very	来 [lái]	come; let
高 [gāo]	high	介绍 [jièshào]	introduce
兴 [xìng]	spirits; interest	一下 [yíxià]	once (to indicate one action)
高兴 [gāoxìng]	glad; happy	这 [zhè]	this
见 [jiàn]	see; meet; view	是 [shì]	be
到 [dào]	arrive; reach; to	李 [Lǐ]	Li (a surname)
请 [qǐng]	please; invite	刘 [Liú]	Liu (a surname)
坐 [zuò]	sit; travel by	先生 [xiānsheng]	mister; Mr.; gentleman; sir
我 [wǒ]	I; me	小姐 [xiǎojiě]	miss; young lady

No problem.
没问题。Méi wèntí.

No problem.
没问题。

Méi wèntí.

OK.
好吧。

Hǎo ba.

You are right!
你是对的！

Nǐ shì duì de!

I agree!
我同意！

Wǒ tóngyì!

Good idea!
好主意！

Hǎo zhǔyi!

Wonderful!
太好了！

Tài hǎo le!

Notes   注解

1. "吧" is used at the end of the sentence, expressing an auxiliary meaning such as proposition, request, order, agreement, approval, guess, or something undecided.

2. "了" is used after verb and adjective as well as at the end of a sentence, indicating the realization of motion and change either in fact or preconception.

3. Chinese words have no morphological changes. The Chinese verb "是 (Zbe)" doesn't have other forms like *am*, *is*, *was*, *been*, etc. This one word "是" functions as all of these forms.

1. "吧" 在句末表示"提议、请求、命令、同意、认可、揣测、未定"等多种辅助意义。

2. "了" 在动词或形容词后边以及句末，表示行动或变化在实际上或预想上的"实现"。

3. 汉语没有"词形变化"。动词"是 (be)"没有 am, is, was, been 之类的形式。

Vocabulary   词语

吧 [ba]	(to indicate consent or request)	同 [tóng]	same; similar; together
没 [méi]	have not	意 [yì]	idea; meaning; intention
问 [wèn]	ask; enquire	同意 [tóngyì]	consent; agree
题 [tí]	title; topic; question	主 [zhǔ]	host; main; advocate
问题 [wèntí]	question; problem	主意 [zhǔyi]	idea; plan; decision
对 1 [duì]	right; correct; true	太 [tài]	excessively; superb
的 1 [de]	(used after an adjective)	了 [le]	(to indicate the realization of a new state)

Don't worry!
别担心！Bié dānxīn!

Don't worry!
别担心！

Bié dānxīn!

It's nothing serious.
问题不大。

Wèntí bú dà.

Just relax.
放松点儿！

Fàngsōng diǎnr!

Don't be nervous.
别紧张！

Bié jǐnzhāng!

No Smoking!
请勿吸烟！

Qǐng wù xī yān!

No Visitors!
游人止步！

Yóurén zhǐbù!

Notes   注解

The imperative sentence is a kind of sentence that makes a request or command, gives advice or warning. The subject of the imperative sentence is absent in Chinese as in English.

"祈使句"表示"请求、命令、劝阻、禁止"等意义。汉语跟英语的"祈使句"通常都不带"主语"。

Vocabulary   词语

别 [bié]	don't	紧张 [jǐnzhāng]	intense; nervous
担 [dān]	undertake; shoulder	勿 [wù]	no; do not
心 [xīn]	heart; mind; core; center	吸 [xī]	inhale; breathe in
担心 [dānxīn]	worry	烟 [yān]	smoke; cigarette
不 [bù]	no; not	游 [yóu]	travel; tour; swim
大 [dà]	big; large; great; old	人 [rén]	person; man; people
放 [fàng]	release; put; let off	游人 [yóurén]	visitor; tourist
松 [sōng]	loosen; relax; pine tree	止 [zhǐ]	stop; halt
点 [diǎn]	point; dot; spot; a bit; o'clock	步 [bù]	step; pace; walk
紧 [jǐn]	tight; taut	止步 [zhǐbù]	stop; go no further
张 [zhāng]	draw; tension; Zhang (a surname)	禁止 [jìnzhǐ]	forbid; ban

Happy birthday!
祝你生日快乐! Zhù nǐ shēngrì kuàilè!

Happy birthday!
祝你生日快乐！

Zhù nǐ shēngrì kuàilè!

Merry Christmas!
圣诞快乐！

Shèngdàn kuàilè!

Happy New Year!
新年快乐！

Xīnnián kuàilè!

Happy Spring Festival!
春节快乐！

Chūn Jié kuàilè!

Wish you the best of health!
祝您健康！

Zhù nín jiànkāng!

Cheers!
干杯！

Gānbēi!

Notes　注解

Chinese people congratulate each other on New Year's Day and the Spring Festival (Chinese Lunar New Year). People also express their best wishes to their friends and relatives at birthday parties.

中国人在春节和新年时互相祝贺。在亲友的生日聚会时，人们向过生日的亲友表示最良好的祝愿。

Vocabulary　词语

祝 [zhù]	wish; best wishes	新 [xīn]	new; fresh
生 [shēng]	life; birth; be born	年 [nián]	year; age
日 [rì]	sun; day	春 [chūn]	spring
生日 [shēngrì]	birthday	节 [jié]	festival
圣 [shèng]	holy; sacred	春节 [Chūn Jié]	Spring Festival (Chinese Lunar New Year)
诞 [dàn]	be born	健 [jiàn]	healthy; strong
圣诞 [Shèngdàn]	Christmas	健康 [jiànkāng]	healthy
快 [kuài]	fast; quick; joyful	干 [gān]	dry; empty
乐 [lè]	pleasure; happy; delight	杯 [bēi]	cup; glass
快乐 [kuàilè]	happy; merry; joyful	干杯 [gānbēi]	drink a toast; cheers

Goodbye!
再见! Zàijiàn!

Goodbye!
再见!

Zàijiàn!

See you later!
回头见!

Huítóu jiàn!

See you tomorrow!
明天见!

Míngtiān jiàn!

Take care!
多保重!

Duō bǎozhòng!

Keep in touch.
保持联系。

Bǎochí liánxì.

Good night!
晚安!

Wǎn' ān!

Notes 注解

"晚上好 (Good evening)!" is used by Chinese people to express greetings when they meet in the evening, while "晚安 (Good night)!" is used to express farewells when they part in the evening. The literal meaning of "晚安" is "wish you a safe night."

中国人在晚上见面时说 "晚上好"，在晚上分别时说 "晚安"。"晚安" 的意思是 "祝你一夜平安"。

Vocabulary 词语

再 [zài]	again; moreover	重 [zhòng]	weight; important
再见 [zàijiàn]	bye	保重 [bǎozhòng]	take care
回 [huí]	return; reply	持 [chí]	hold; maintain
头 [tóu]	head; top; beginning	保持 [bǎochí]	keep; maintain
回头 [huítóu]	later; turn one's head	联 [lián]	connect; unite
明 [míng]	bright; next	系 [xì]	tie; relate; series; linking
天 [tiān]	sky; day; weather	联系 [liánxì]	contact; relate; keep in touch
明天 [míngtiān]	tomorrow	安 [ān]	safe; peaceful; install
多 [duō]	many; much; excessive	平安 [píng' ān]	safe and sound
保 [bǎo]	protect; defend; keep	晚安 [wǎn' ān]	good night

How are you?
您好吗? Nín hǎo ma?

Fine, and you?
很好，您呢? Hěn hǎo, nín ne?

How are you?		Fine, and you?	
您好吗？	Nín hǎo ma?	很好，您呢？	Hěn hǎo, nín ne?
How has everything been recently?		Not bad.	
最近怎么样？	Zuìjìn zěnmeyàng?	还行。	Hái xíng.
Thank you!		You are welcome!	
谢谢你！	Xièxie nǐ!	别客气！	Bié kèqi!
Sorry!		Never mind!	
对不起！	Duìbuqǐ!	没关系！	Méi guānxi!
Excuse me!		It's nothing!	
请原谅！	Qǐng yuánliàng!	没什么！	Méi shénme!

Notes　注解

1. The right columns from sentence frames 007 to 010 are the most appropriate responses to the left ones.
2. In Chinese, a yes-no question is formed by adding "吗" at the end of the sentence. In general "是的 (Yes)" or "不 (No)" is not used to answer the question first as in English.
3. "呢" is used at the end of the sentence to show the interrogative mood. The frame "N (noun or pronoun) + 呢" means "What about N?" or "Where is N?"

1. 从句式 007 到 010，"右栏"都是对"左栏"的最合适的回应。
2. "吗"在句末表示"疑问"，构成"是非问句"，但却不像英语必须先使用"是的 (Yes)"或"不 (No)"回答问题。
3. "呢"在句末表示"疑问"，句式"N (名词或代词) + 呢"的意思是"N 怎么样？"或"N 在哪里？"。

Vocabulary　词语

吗 [ma]	(to form a question)	客 [kè]	guest; customer
呢 [ne]	(to form a question)	客气 [kèqi]	polite; modest
最 [zuì]	most; in the first place	对不起 [duìbuqǐ]	sorry
最近 [zuìjìn]	recently	关系 [guānxi]	relation
怎么样 [zěnmeyàng]	how; what is it like	没关系 [méi guānxi]	never mind
还 [hái]	still; yet; even; fairly	原谅 [yuánliàng]	excuse; forgive
谢谢 [xièxie]	thank	没什么 [méi shénme]	nothing

May I come in?
我可以进来吗? Wǒ kěyǐ jìnlái ma?

Come in, please!
请进! Qǐng jìn!

May I come in?		Come in, please!	
我可以进来吗?	Wǒ kěyǐ jìnlái ma?	请进!	Qǐng jìn!
Are you Manager Wang?		Yes, I am.	
你是王经理吗?	Nǐ shì Wáng jīnglǐ ma?	对,我是。	Duì, wǒ shì.
This is my name card.		Thanks.	
这是我的名片。	Zhè shì wǒ de míngpiàn.	谢谢。	Xièxie!
Could you do me a favor?		Of course.	
你能帮帮我吗?	Nǐ néng bāngbang wǒ ma?	当然。	Dāngrán.
Do you know that?		No, I don't know.	
您知道吗?	Nín zhīdào ma?	不,我不知道。	Bù, wǒ bù zhīdào.

Notes　注解

1. In Chinese, the word order of the interrogative sentence formed by adding the sinogram "吗" is the same with the declarative sentence, namely "a yes-no interrogative sentence = a declarative sentence + "吗"".

2. The duplicate form "VV" shows a short time action or a tentative action. "帮帮 [bāngbang]" means "帮一下 [bāng yíxià] (to help a bit)".

3. "不 (not)" is used before verbs and adjectives to indicate negation. "不 (No)" at the beginning of the answer indicates the opposite meaning of the interrogative sentence.

1. "吗"构成的"是非疑问句",语序跟"叙述句"相同,即:"是非疑问句＝叙述句＋吗"。

2. 动词重叠"VV"表示做一次短暂的动作或尝试性的动作。"帮帮"的意思是"帮一下"。

3. "不 (not)"在"动词、形容词"之前表示否定。答句句首的"不 (No)"表示跟问句的意思相反。

Vocabulary　词语

可以 [kěyǐ]	may; can; OK; approve	片 [piàn]	card; flat; film
进 [jìn]	enter; into	名片 [míngpiàn]	name card
进来 [jìnlái]	come in	能 [néng]	can; be able to
经理 [jīnglǐ]	manager	帮 [bāng]	help; aid; assist
对2 [duì]	yes	当然 [dāngrán]	of course
的2 [de]	(used after a noun to indicate possession)	知 [zhī]	know; knowledge
名 [míng]	name; famous; well-known	知道 [zhīdào]	know

I'd better go.

我该走了。 Wǒ gāi zǒu le?

Won't you stay a little longer?
再坐一会儿吧! Zài zuò yíhuìr ba!

I'd better go.		Won't you stay a little longer?	
我该走了。	Wǒ gāi zǒu le.	再坐一会儿吧!	Zài zuò yíhuìr ba!
It's getting late.		It's still quite early.	
时间不早了。	Shíjiān bù zǎo le.	还早着呢。	Hái zǎo zhene.
I have got something else to do.		Do come again.	
我还有点儿事。	Wǒ hái yǒu diǎnr shì.	以后常来呀。	Yǐhòu cháng lái ya.
Take good care of yourself!		Let me see you out.	
您多保重!	Nín duō bǎozhòng!	我送送你。	Wǒ sòngsong nǐ.
You don't need to see me out!		Call me later.	
别送了。	Bié sòng le.	回头给我打电话。	Huítóu gěi wǒ dǎ diànhuà.

Notes   注解

1. "没" means "没有 (have not)", expressing the negation of possession, existence, and experience.
2. The pronunciation of "会儿" in the phrase "一会儿" is not two syllables [huì er], but one syllable [huìr].

1. "没" 的意思是 "没有"，表示对 "领有、存在、经历" 的否定。
2. "一会儿" 的 "会儿" 在语音上不是两个音节 [huì er]，而是一个音节 [huìr]。

Vocabulary   词语

时间 [shíjiān]	time	常 [cháng]	often; usually; ordinary
着呢 [zhene]	quite	经常 [jīngcháng]	often; frequently
该 [gāi]	should; owe	呀 [ya]（叹词）	(interjection)
应该 [yīnggāi]	should; ought to	送 [sòng]	deliver; see sb. off; give a gift
一会儿 [yíhuìr]	a little while; in a moment	给 [gěi]	give; for; to
有 [yǒu]	have; there be	打 [dǎ]	host; main; hit; make (a call)
事 [shì]	matter; thing; affair	电 [diàn]	electricity; electric
后 [hòu]	behind; after; empress	话 [huà]	talk; spoken words
以后 [yǐhòu]	after; later	电话 [diànhuà]	telephone; phone call

You are really terrific!
你真了不起! Nǐ zhēn liǎobuqǐ!

You are overpraising me.
您过奖了。 Nín guòjiǎng le.

You are really terrific!	**You are overpraising me.**
你真了不起！　　Nǐ zhēn liǎobuqǐ!	您过奖了。　　Nín guòjiǎng le.
Your boyfriend is so handsome!	**Not at all.**
你的男友真帅！　Nǐ de nányǒu zhēn shuài.	哪里哪里。　　Nǎli nǎli.
Your sweater is so pretty!	**It's not that pretty.**
你的毛衣真好看！ Nǐ de máoyī zhēn hǎokàn!	哪里，有什么好看。Nǎli, yǒu shénme hǎokàn.
You sing so well!	**It still falls far short.**
你唱得太好了！　Nǐ chàng de tài hǎo le!	还差得远呢。　　Hái chà de yuǎn ne.

Notes　注解

Chinese people are usually very modest. When being praised, they always say "您过奖了", "哪里哪里", "还差得远呢" instead of saying "谢谢" directly.

中国人通常很谦虚。当受到夸奖时，他们总是说"您过奖了"、"哪里哪里"、"还差得远呢"，而不是说"谢谢"。

Vocabulary　词语

真 [zhēn]	true; real; indeed		衣服 [yīfu]	clothes
了不起 [liǎobuqǐ]	terrific; extraordinary		好看 [hǎokàn]	good-looking; pretty; beautiful
过 [guò]	pass; over; excessively		哪 [nǎ]	which; what
奖 [jiǎng]	praise; award; prize		里 [lǐ]	place; inside; in
过奖 [guòjiǎng]	overpraise		哪里 [nǎli]	where
男 [nán]	male; son		那 [nà]	that
男孩儿 [nánháir]	boy		那里 [nàli]	there
男友 [nányǒu]	boyfriend		这里 [zhèli]	here
帅 [shuài]	handsome		唱 [chàng]	sing
女 [nǚ]	female; daughter		得 [de]	(used after a verb to introduce a result)
女孩儿 [nǚháir]	girl		差 [chà]	differ from; fall short off
女友 [nǚyǒu]	girlfriend		远 [yuǎn]	far

Persons and Things

人和物 [rén hé wù]

011. What is this? 这是什么？   This is a textbook. 这是课本。

012. Who is she? 她是谁？   She is Manager Wang. 她是王经理。

013. Whose cell phone is this? 这是谁的手机？   That is my cell phone. 那是我的手机。

014. Who has a camera? 谁有相机？   He has a camera. 他有相机。

015. What is there on the table? 桌子上有什么？   There is a pictorial on the table. 桌子上有画报。

016. Where are the newspapers? 报纸在哪里？   The newspapers are on the bookshelf. 报纸在书架上。

017. Which country are you from? 你是哪国人？   I am German. 我是德国人。

018. What is your family name? 您姓什么？   My family name is Wang. 我姓王。

019. What is your name? 您叫什么？   My name is Wang Aihua. 我叫王爱华。

020. How old are you? 您多大年纪了？   I am 67 years old. 我六十七了。

What is this?
这是什么？ Zhè shì shénme?

This is a textbook.
这是课本。 Zhè shì kèběn.

① Subjective 主体	② Linking 联系	③ Relative 系体
this 这 [zhè]		what 什么 [shénme]
these 这些 [zhèxiē]		textbook 课本 [kèběn]
that 那 [nà]	be 是 [shì]	notebook 本子 [běnzi]
those 那些 [nàxiē]		bookshelf 书架 [shūjià]
Sentence Making 造句 [zàojù]	What are those? Those are bookshelves.	那些是什么？ 那些是书架。

Notes　注解

1. In Chinese, the frame of "是 [shì]" sentence is "subjective + be + relative".
2. Chinese words have no single or plural forms except nouns that indicate people and personal pronouns.
3. "这 [zhè] (this)" indicates objects near the speaker; "那 [nà] (that)" indicates objects far from the speaker; "哪 [nǎ] (which)" and "什么 [shénme] (what)" indicate something unknown.

1. 汉语"是"字句的框架是"主体＋是＋系体"。
2. 汉语除了指人的名词和人称代词之外，"单数"和"复数"具有同一的形式。
3. "这"指代较近的事物；"那"指代较远的事物；"哪"和"什么"指代未知的事物。

Vocabulary　词语

这 [zhè]	this	书 [shū]; 书本 [shūběn]	book
这些 [zhèxiē]	these	课 [kè]	lesson; text
那 [nà]	that	课本 [kèběn]	textbook
那些 [nàxiē]	those	本子 [běnzi]	notebook
哪 [nǎ]	which	桌子 [zhuōzi]	table
哪些 [nǎxiē]	which	书桌 [shūzhuō]; 课桌 [kèzhuō]	desk
什么 [shénme]	what	书架 [shūjià]	bookshelf

Who is she?
她是谁？ Tā shì shuí?

She is Manager Wang.
她是王经理。 Tā shì Wáng jīnglǐ.

①	②	③	
Subjective 主 体	Linking 联 系	Relative 系体	
		Family Name 姓	Term of Address 称谓
she 她 [tā]		who谁[shuí]	
		Wang 王 [Wáng]	manager 经理 [jīnglǐ]
	be 是 [shì]	Li 李 [Lǐ]	professor 教授 [jiàoshòu]
he 他 [tā]		Chen 陈 [Chén]	aunt 阿姨 [āyí]
Sentence Making 造句 [zàojù]	Who is he? He is Professor Chen.	他是谁？ 他是陈教授。	

Notes　注解

1. "谁 [shuí/shéi] (who)" indicates people unknown. "谁" can be used to indicate either what people or which people.
2. The general way Chinese people address a person is "family name + title (position, status, occupation, reationship, etc.)"

1. "谁" 指未知的人。"谁" 可以表示 "什么人"；也可以表示 "哪些人"。
2. 中国人对于 "人" 的称呼，一般为 "姓 + 称谓 (职务、尊称、身份、亲属等)"。

Vocabulary　词语

谁 [shuí/shéi]	who	经理 [jīnglǐ]	manager
你 [nǐ]	you	教授 [jiàoshòu]	professor
您 [nín]	you (with respect)	主任 [zhǔrèn]	director
你们 [nǐmen]	you	老师 [lǎoshī]	teacher
我 [wǒ]	I; me	先生 [xiānsheng]	mister
我们 [wǒmen]	we; us	女士 [nǚshì]	madam
他 [tā]	he; him	大姐 [dà jiě]	elder sister
她 [tā]	she; her	大哥 [dà gē]	elder brother
它 [tā]	it	叔叔 [shūshu]	uncle (at one's father's age)
他们 [tāmen]	they; them	阿姨 [āyí]	aunt (at one's mother's age)

013 Whose cell phone is this?
这是谁的手机？ Zhè shì shuí de shǒujī?

That is my cell phone.
那是我的手机。 Nà shì wǒ de shǒujī.

① Subjective 主体	② Linking 联系	③ Relative 系体	
this 这 [zhè] that 那 [nà]		whose 谁的 [shuí de] my 我的 [wǒ de] her 她的 [tā de]	cell phone 手机 [shǒujī] watch 手表 [shǒubiǎo] scarf 围巾 [wéijīn]
	be(is) 是 [shì]		
this cell phone 这个手机 [zhège shǒujī] that scarf 那个围巾 [nàge wéijīn]		whose 谁的 [shuí de] mine 我的 [wǒ de] hers 她的 [tā de]	
Sentence Making 造句 [zàojù]	Whose is that scarf? That scarf is hers.	那个围巾是谁的? 那个围巾是她的。	

Notes 注解

1. "的 [de]" is added after "男 [nán] (male)" or "女 [nǚ] (female)" to indicate man or woman.
2. Pronouns with "的 [de]" behind them can function as possessive determiners and possessive pronouns, so there aren't special words indicating *my* and *mine* in Chinese as there are in English.
1. "的" 加在 "男" 或 "女" 之后表示 "男人" 或 "女人"。
2. "的" 加在 "人称代词" 之后就是 "物主代词"，但是汉语没有英语那种 my 和 mine 的区分。

Vocabulary 词语

谁的 [shuí de]	whose	提包 [tíbāo]	handbag
我的 [wǒ de]	my; mine	钱包 [qiánbāo]	purse
你的 [nǐ de]	your; yours	钥匙 [yàoshi]	key
他的 [tā de]	his	钢笔 [gāngbǐ]	pen
她的 [tā de]	her; hers	手机 [shǒujī]	cell phone
它的 [tā de]	its	手表 [shǒubiǎo]	watch
我们的 [wǒmen de]	our; ours	手帕 [shǒupà]	handkerchief
你们的 [nǐmen de]	your; yours	帽子 [màozi]	hat
他们的 [tāmen de]	their; theirs	围巾 [wéijīn]	scarf

Who has a camera?
谁有相机？ Shuí yǒu xiàngjī?

He has a camera.
他有相机。 Tā yǒu xiàngjī.

① Subjective 主体	② Possessing 领有	③ Belongings 属物
who 谁 [shuí]		camera 相机 [xiàngjī]
he 他 [tā]		cell phone 手机 [shǒujī]
my friend 我的朋友 [wǒ de péngyou]	have/has 有 [yǒu]	recorder 录音机 [lùyīnjī]
his elder brother 他的哥哥 [tā de gēge]		microphone 扩音器 [kuòyīnqì]
his teacher 他的老师 [tā de lǎoshī]		vacuum cleaner 吸尘器 [xīchénqì]
Sentence Making 造句 [zàojù]	Who has a car? He has a car.	谁有汽车? 他有汽车。

Notes 注解

1. The meaning of Chinese "有 [yǒu]" in this sentence frame is "possessing." It is equivalent to "have" in English.
2. In Chinese, words are formed by sinograms. The most common words forming module is "sinograms that stand for features + sinograms that stand for categories". For example, "机 [jī] (machinery)" and "器 [qì] (appliance)" are both "sinograms that stand for categories".

1. 汉语 "有" 在本表中的意思为 "领有 (possessing)"，对应于英语 "have"。
2. 汉语以字构词,最常见的是 "特征字＋类别字"。如 "机 (machinery)" 和 "器 (appliance)" 都是 "类别字"。

Vocabulary 词语

机 [jī]	machinery	器 [qì]	appliance; instrument
耳机 [ěrjī]	earphone	电器 [diànqì]	electrical appliance
手机 [shǒujī]	cell phone	乐器 [yuèqì]	musical instrument
相机 [xiàngjī]	camera	容器 [róngqì]	container
摄像机 [shèxiàngjī]	video camera	助听器 [zhùtīngqì]	hearing aid
录音机 [lùyīnjī]	recorder	吸尘器 [xīchénqì]	vacuum cleaner
打印机 [dǎyìnjī]	printer	扩音器 [kuòyīnqì]	microphone
复印机 [fùyìnjī]	copier	调压器 [tiáoyāqì]	voltage regulator

What is there on the table?
桌子上有什么？ Zhuōzi shang yǒu shénme?

There is a pictorial on the table.
桌子上有画报。 Zhuōzi shang yǒu huàbào.

Location 地点 ①		Existing 存在 ②	Subjective 主体 ③
table 桌子 [zhuōzi]			what 什么 [shénme]
bookshelf 书架 [shūjià]			pictorial 画报 [huàbào]
desk 书桌 [shūzhuō]	on 上 [shàng]	there be 有 [yǒu]	newspaper 报纸 [bàozhǐ]
cabinet 柜子 [guìzi]			dictionary 字典 [zìdiǎn]
chair 椅子 [yǐzi]			notebook 本子 [běnzi]
Sentence Making 造句 [zàojù]	What is there on the chair? There are newspapers on the chair.		椅子上有什么？ 椅子上有报纸。

Notes 注解

1. The meaning of Chinese "有 [yǒu]" in this sentence frame is "existing". It is equivalent to (there) be (is/are) in English.
2. Chinese "上 [shàng] (on)" used after nouns indicates the surface of things. "N + 上 [shàng]" is often used to express the location where other objects exist. In the following left table are objects which can precede the word "上 [shàng]." In the right table are those which can exist on the surface of other objects.
1. 汉语 "有" 在本表中的意思为 "存在 (existing)"，对应于英语 "there be"。
2. 汉语 "上 (on)" 加在名词之后表示某物体的表面。通常成为另一物体 "存在 (existing)" 的 "地点 (location)"。
   下列左表为具有表面，词后可加 "上" 字的物体；右表为可以附着在前一物体表面 "上" 的另一物体。

Vocabulary 词语

柜台 [guìtái]	counter	报纸 [bàozhǐ]	newspaper
展台 [zhǎntái]	exhibition platform	画报 [huàbào]	pictorial
墙 [qiáng]	wall	招贴画 [zhāotiēhuà]	pictorial poster
橱窗 [chúchuāng]	show window	广告画 [guǎnggàohuà]	poster
画廊 [huàláng]	gallery	图片 [túpiàn]	picture
报栏 [bào lán]	newspaper column	照片 [zhàopiàn]	photograph
宣传栏 [xuānchuán lán]	bulletin board	地图 [dìtú]	map
布告栏 [bùgào lán]	billboard	图表 [túbiǎo]	chart

Where are the newspapers?
报纸在哪里？ Bàozhǐ zài nǎli?

The newspapers are on the bookshelf.
报纸在书架上。 Bàozhǐ zài shūjià shang.

① Subjective 主体	② Existing 存在	③ Location 地点	
newspaper 报纸 [bàozhǐ]		where 哪里 [nǎli]	
pictorial 画报 [huàbào]	be 在 [zài]	bookshelf 书架 [shūjià]	on 上 [shàng]
dictionary 字典 [zìdiǎn]		desk 书桌 [shūzhuō]	
table 桌子 [zhuōzi]		classroom 教室 [jiàoshì]	in 里 [lǐ]
closet 柜子 [guìzi]		bedroom 卧室 [wòshì]	
Sentence Making 造句 [zàojù]	Where are the closets? The closets are in the bedroom.	柜子在哪里？ 柜子在寝室里。	

Notes 注解

1. The meaning of Chinese "在 [zài]" in this sentence frame is "existing", it is equivalent to " be + preposition (like on, in, etc.)" in English.
2. "里 [lǐ] (in)" used after nouns indicates the inside space of objectives. "N + 里 [lǐ]" is often used to express the location where other objects exist. In the following left table are objects which can be added before the word "里 [lǐ]". In the right table are those which exist inside the space of other objects.
1. "在" 在本表中义为 "存在（existing）"，对应于英语 "be"。
2. "里 (in)" 在名词之后表示某实体空间边界之内，通常成为另一物体 "存在" 的 "地点"。下列的左表为具有空间边界，词后可加 "里" 字的实体；右表为可以位于前一实体空间边界 "里" 的另一物体。

Vocabulary 词语

室 [shì]；房间 [fángjiān]	room	桌子 [zhuōzi]	table
卧室 [wòshì]	bedroom	案子 [ànzi]	chopping board
教室 [jiàoshì]	classroom	椅子 [yǐzi]	chair
画室 [huàshì]	studio	凳子 [dèngzi]	stool
休息室 [xiūxishì]	lounge; lobby	柜子 [guìzi]	cupboard; cabinet; closet
医务室 [yīwùshì]	clinic	箱子 [xiāngzi]	case; chest
实验室 [shíyànshì]	laboratory	盒子 [hézi]	box

Which country are you from?
你是哪国人？ Nǐ shì nǎ guó rén?

I am German.
我是德国人。 Wǒ shì Déguórén.

	① Subjective 主体	② Linking 联系	③ Relative 系体
	you 您 [nín]		from which country 哪国人 [nǎ guó rén]
	you 你 [nǐ]		German 德国人 [Déguórén]
	I 我 [wǒ]	be 是 [shì]	American 美国人 [Měiguórén]
	that person 那个人 [nàge rén]		Chinese 中国人 [Zhōngguórén]
	her friend 她的朋友 [tā de péngyou]		French 法国人 [Fǎguórén]
Sentence Making 造句 [zàojù]	Which country are you from? I am French.		你是哪国人？ 我是法国人。

Notes 注解

The left and right tables show names of the countries and people from those countries respectively.
下面的表中，左边是"国家"，右边是"这个国家的人"。

Vocabulary 词语

中国 [Zhōngguó]	China	中国人 [Zhōngguórén]	Chinese
美国 [Měiguó]	America	美国人 [Měiguórén]	American
法国 [Fǎguó]	France	法国人 [Fǎguórén]	French
德国 [Déguó]	Germany	德国人 [Déguérén]	German
意大利 [Yìdàlì]	Italy	意大利人 [Yìdàlìrén]	Italian
西班牙 [Xībānyá]	Spain	西班牙人 [Xībānyárén]	Spanish
俄罗斯 [Éluósī]	Russia	俄罗斯人 [Éluósīrén]	Russian
加拿大 [Jiānádà]	Canada	加拿大人 [Jiānádàrén]	Canadian
印度 [Yìndù]	India	印度人 [Yìndùrén]	Indian
日本 [Rìběn]	Japan	日本人 [Rìběnrén]	Japanese
韩国 [Hánguó]	South Korea	韩国人 [Hánguórén]	Korean

您姓什么？ Nín xìng shénme?

My family name is Wang.

我姓王。 Wǒ xìng Wáng.

①	②	③
Subjective 主体	Linking 联系	Relative 系体
your 您 [nín]		what 什么 [shénme]
my 我 [wǒ]		Wang 王 [Wáng]
your 你 [nǐ]	family name is 姓 [xìng]	Li 李 [Lǐ]
his 他 [tā]		Chen 陈 [chén]
her 她 [tā]		Liu 刘 [Liú]
Sentence Making 造句 [zàojù]	What is her family name? Her family name is Liu.	她姓什么？ 她姓刘。

Notes 注解

1. Generally Chinese people will ask each other's family name on their first meeting. When confronted with those who are elder or have a higher position and more knowledge, "您贵姓 [nín guìxìng]?" should be used to show respect.

2. The ten most common family names in China are shown in the left table. Also, the nine family names related to some famous Chinese people in the twentieth century are shown in the right table.

1. 中国人初次见面，一般先问姓，对于年长或比自己职位、学识高的人，则要用"您贵姓？"来询句，以示尊敬。

2. 下面的左表是中国人最常见的 9 个姓。右表是跟二十世纪著名华人有关的 9 个姓。

李 [Lǐ]	Li	孙 [Sūn]	Sun	孙中山 [Sūn Zhōngshān]	Sun Zhongshan (Sun Yat-sen)
王 [Wáng]	Wang	毛 [Máo]	Mao	毛泽东 [Máo Zédōng]	Mao Zedong
张 [Zhāng]	Zhang	周 [Zhōu]	Zhou	周恩来 [Zhōu Ēnlái]	Zhou Enlai
刘 [Liú]	Liu	朱 [Zhū]	Zhu	朱德 [Zhū Dé]	Zhu De
陈 [Chén]	Chen	邓 [Dèng]	Deng	邓小平 [Dèng Xiǎopíng]	Deng Xiaoping
杨 [Yáng]	Yang	鲁 [Lǔ]	Lu	鲁迅 [Lǔ Xùn]	Lu Xun
赵 [Zhào]	Zhao	茅 [Máo]	Mao	茅盾 [Máo Dùn]	Mao Dun
黄 [Huáng]	Huang	郭 [Guō]	Guo	郭沫若 [Guō Mòruò]	Guo Moruo
徐 [Xú]	Xu	曹 [Cáo]	Cao	曹禺 [Cáo Yú]	Cao Yu

What is your name?
您叫什么？ Nín jiào shénme?

My name is Wang Aihua.
我叫王爱华。 Wǒ jiào Wáng Àihuá.

① Subjective 主体	② Linking 联系	③ Relative 系体
your 您 [nín]		what 什么 [shénme]
your 你 [nǐ]		Wang Aihua 王爱华 [Wáng Àihuá]
my 我 [wǒ]	name is 叫 [jiào]	Li Dayong 李大勇 [Lǐ Dàyǒng]
his 他 [tā]		Chen Fen 陈芬 [Chén Fēn]
her 她 [tā]		Liu Fang 刘芳 [Liú Fāng]
Sentence Making 造句 [zàojù]	What is her name? Her name is Liu Fang.	她叫什么？ 她叫刘芳。

Notes 注解

1. The structure of Chinese name is "family name + given name". Most of the family names are one sinogram. Only a few are two sinograms, such as "诸葛 [Zhūgě], 公孙 [Gōngsūn]".
2. The following 18 names are known well in China. They are from famous novels: *The Romance of the Three Kingdoms* and *Heroes of the Marshes*.
1. 中国人是："姓 + 名"。"姓"绝大多数是一个字，个别的是两个字 (诸葛、公孙)。
2. 下面的表中是中国人家喻户晓的 18 个人名，分别是著名小说《三国演义》和《水浒传》中的人名。

诸葛亮 [Zhūgě Liàng]	Zhuge Liang	宋江 [Sòng Jiāng]	Song Jiang
刘备 [Liú Bèi]	Liu Bei	卢俊义 [Lú Jùnyì]	Lu Junyi
关羽 [Guān Yǔ]	Guan Yu	吴用 [Wú Yòng]	Wu Yong
张飞 [Zhāng Fēi]	Zhang Fei	公孙胜 [Gōngsūn Shèng]	Gongsun Sheng
赵云 [Zhào Yún]	Zhao Yun	林冲 [Lín Chōng]	Lin Chong
曹操 [Cáo Cāo]	Cao Cao	杨志 [Yáng Zhì]	Yang Zhi
孙权 [Sūn Quán]	Sun Quan	李逵 [Lǐ Kuí]	Li Kui
周瑜 [Zhōu Yú]	Zhou Yu	鲁智深 [Lǔ Zhìshēn]	Lu Zhishen
吕布 [Lǚ Bù]	Lü Bu	武松 [Wǔ Sōng]	Wu Song

How old are you?

您多大年纪了？ Nín duō dà niánjì le?

I am 67 years old.

我六十七了。 Wǒ liùshíqī le.

	① Subjective 主体	② Linking 联系	③ Relative 系体	④ Postpositive 后助词
	you 您 [nín]		how old 多大年纪 [duō dà niánjì]	
	I 我 [wǒ]		67 years old 六十七 [liùshíqī]	
	you 你 [nǐ]	be { 是 [shì] }	how old 多大 [duō dà]	{ } 了 [le]
	I 我 [wǒ]		34 years old 三十四岁 [sānshísì suì]	
	that boy 那个男孩儿 [nàge nánháir]		how old 几岁 [jǐ suì]	
	he 他 [tā]		9 years old 九岁 [jiǔ suì]	
Sentence Making 造句 [zàojù]	How old is he ? He is 7 years old.		他几岁了？ 他七岁了。	

Numbers in Chinese (0-99)　汉语的数目(0-99)

零 [líng]	zero
一 [yī]	one
二 [èr]	two
三 [sān]	three
四 [sì]	four
五 [wǔ]	five
六 [liù]	six
七 [qī]	seven
八 [bā]	eight
九 [jiǔ]	nine
十 [shí]	ten

0 零	1 一	2 二	3 三	4 四	5 五	6 六	7 七	8 八	9 九
10 十	11 十一	12 十二	13 十三	14 十四	15 十五	16 十六	17 十七	18 十八	19 十九
20 二十	21 二十一	22 二十二	23 二十三	24 二十四	25 二十五	26 二十六	27 二十七	28 二十八	29 二十九
30 三十	31 三十一	32 三十二	33 三十三	34 三十四	35 三十五	36 三十六	37 三十七	38 三十八	39 三十九
40 四十	41 四十一	42 四十二	43 四十三	44 四十四	45 四十五	46 四十六	47 四十七	48 四十八	49 四十九
50 五十	51 五十一	52 五十二	53 五十三	54 五十四	55 五十五	56 五十六	57 五十七	58 五十八	59 五十九
60 六十	61 六十一	62 六十二	63 六十三	64 六十四	65 六十五	66 六十六	67 六十七	68 六十八	69 六十九
70 七十	71 七十一	72 七十二	73 七十三	74 七十四	75 七十五	76 七十六	77 七十七	78 七十八	79 七十九
80 八十	81 八十一	82 八十二	83 八十三	84 八十四	85 八十五	86 八十六	87 八十七	88 八十八	89 八十九
90 九十	91 九十一	92 九十二	93 九十三	94 九十四	95 九十五	96 九十六	97 九十七	98 九十八	99 九十九

Time and Location

时间和地点 [shíjiān hé dìdiǎn]

021. What is the date today? 今天几号？   It is May the eighth today. 今天五月八号。

022. What day is it today? 今天星期几？   It is Thursday today. 今天星期四。

023. What time is it? 现在是什么时间？   It is ten o'clock. 现在是十点。

024. When do you get up? 你什么时候起床？   I get up at 6 in the morning. 我早晨六点起床。

025. What people did you see in the park yesterday? 您昨天在公园看见一些什么人？

     I saw many foreign tourists in the park yesterday. 我昨天在公园看见许多外国游客。

026. Where is the washroom? 洗手间在哪里？   The washroom is on the second floor. 洗手间在二楼。

027. What are there in the sky? 天空中有什么？   There are clouds in the sky. 天空中有云。

028. What books does the library have? 图书馆有一些什么书？

     The library has many books written in foreign languages. 图书馆有许多外文书。

029. What time shall we meet? 我们什么时候见面？

     We shall meet at half past three tomorrow afternoon. 我们明天下午三点半见面。

030. Where will you wait for me tomorrow? 你明天在哪里等我？

     I'll wait for you at the gate of the cinema tomorrow. 我明天在电影院门口等你。

What is the date today?

今天几号？ Jīntiān jǐ hào?

It is May the eighth today.

今天五月八号。 Jīntiān Wǔyuè bā hào.

	①	②	③	
			Relative 系体	
	Subjective 主体	Linking 联系	which month 哪个月份	which day 哪一天
	today 今天 [jīntiān]		What day of the month (date) 几号 [jǐ hào]	
	tomorrow 明天 [míngtiān]	is { 是 [shì] }	May 五月 [Wǔyuè] August 八月 [Bāyuè] December 十二月 [Shí' èryuè]	the eighth 八号 [bā hào] the ninth 九号 [jiǔ hào] the twentieth 二十号 [èrshí hào]
	next Monday 下周一 [xià zhōuyī]			
Sentence Making 造句 [zàojù]	What is the date next Monday? Next Monday is December the twentieth.		下周一是几号？ 下周一是十二月二十号。	

Notes 注解

In Chinese, "一月 (January)" means "the first month of the year"；"二月 (February)" means "the second month of the year".
汉语 "一月" 的意思是 "每年的第一个月"；"二月" 的意思是 "每年的第二个月"。

Vocabulary 词语

天 [tiān]	sky; day	月 [yuè]	moon; month
今天 [jīntiān]	today	一月 [Yīyuè]	January
明天 [míngtiān]	tomorrow	二月 [Èryuè]	February
后天 [hòutiān]	the day after tomorrow	三月 [Sānyuè]	March
大后天 [dàhòutiān]	three days from now	四月 [Sìyuè]	April
昨天 [zuótiān]	yesterday	五月 [Wǔyuè]	May
前天 [qiántiān]	the day before yesterday	六月 [Liùyuè]	June
大前天 [dàqiántiān]	three days ago	七月 [Qīyuè]	July
半天 [bàntiān]	half of the day	八月 [Bāyuè]	August
前半天 [qián bàntiān]	forenoon	九月 [Jiǔyuè]	September
后半天 [hòu bàntiān]	afternoon	十月 [Shíyuè]	October
全天 [quán tiān]	all day	十一月 [Shíyīyuè]	November
每天 [měi tiān]	every day	十二月 [Shí'èryuè]	December

What day is it today?
今天星期几？ Jīntiān xīngqī jǐ?

It is Thursday today.
今天星期四。 Jīntiān Xīngqīsì.

① Subjective 主体	② Linking 联系	③ Relative 系体
today 今天 [jīntiān]		what day of the week 星期几 [xīngqī jǐ]
tomorrow 明天 [míngtiān]		Thursday 星期四 [Xīngqīsì]
July the third 七月三号 [Qīyuè sān hào]	is {是 [shì]}	Sunday 星期天 [Xīngqītiān]
your birthday 你的生日 [nǐ de shēngrì]		Monday 星期一 [Xīngqīyī]
Sentence Making 造句 [zàojù]	What day is your birthday? My birthday is Monday.	你的生日是星期几？ 我的生日是星期一。

Notes 注解

In Chinese, "星期一 (Monday)" means the first working day of the week; "星期二 (Tuesday)" means the second working day of the week.

汉语"星期一"的意思是"每星期工作日的第一天"；"星期二"的意思是"每星期工作日的第二天"。

Vocabulary 词语

日 [rì]	/	sun; day
星期 [xīngqī]	周 [zhōu]	week
星期日 [Xīngqīrì]; 星期天 [xīngqītiān]	周日 [zhōurì]	Sunday
星期一 [Xīngqīyī]	周一 [zhōuyī]	Monday
星期二 [Xīngqī'èr]	周二 [zhōu'èr]	Tuesday
星期三 [Xīngqīsān]	周三 [zhōusān]	Wednesday
星期四 [Xīngqīsì]	周四 [zhōusì]	Thursday
星期五 [Xīngqīwǔ]	周五 [zhōuwǔ]	Friday
星期六 [Xīngqīliù]	周六 [zhōuliù]	Saturday
/	周末 [zhōumò]	weekend
上星期 [shàng xīngqī]	上周 [shàng zhōu]	last week
下星期 [xià xīngqī]	下周 [xià zhōu]	next week

What time is it?
现在是什么时间？ Xiànzài shì shénme shíjiān?

It is ten o'clock.
现在是十点。 Xiànzài shì shí diǎn.

① Subjective 主体	② Linking 联系	③ Relative 系体
it 现在 [xiànzài] the arrival time at the last stop of this train 这趟车到达终点的时间 [zhè tàng chē dàodá zhōngdiǎn de shíjiān] the opening ceremony 开幕式 [kāimùshì]	is { 是 [shì]}	what time 什么时间 [shénme shíjiān] ten o'clock 十点 [shí diǎn] half past six in the evening 晚上六点半 [wǎnshang liù diǎn bàn] 明天上午九点 [míngtiān shàngwǔ jiǔ diǎn] nine tomorrow morning
Sentence Making 造句 [zàojù]	What time is the opening ceremony? The opening ceremony is at nine tomorrow morning.	开幕式是什么时间？ 开幕式是明天上午九点。

Notes 注解

In Chinese, the order of *temporal words* is from words expressing longer temporal concepts to words expressing shorter temporal concepts: "century, year, month, day, hour, minute, second".

汉语表示"时间"的词语按照"从大到小"的顺序排列。依次是"世纪→年→月→日→时→分→秒"。

Vocabulary 词语

世纪 [shìjì]	century	时间 [shíjiān]	time
本世纪 [běn shìjì]	this century	时钟 [shízhōng]	clock
上个世纪 [shàng ge shìjì]	last century	点 [diǎn];（小）时 [(xiǎo)shí]	hour
下个世纪 [xià ge shìjì]	next century	半 [bàn]	half
年 [nián]	year	半小时 [bàn xiǎoshí]	half an hour
今年 [jīnnián]	this year	刻 [kè]	quarter
去年 [qùnián]	last year	分 [fēn]	minute
前年 [qiánnián]	the year before last	秒 [miǎo]	second
明年 [míngnián]	next year	三点五十分 [sān diǎn wǔshí fēn]	three fifty
后年 [hòunián]	the year after next	四点差十分 [sì diǎn chà shí fēn]	ten to four
时期 [shíqī]	period; stage	六点半 [liù diǎn bàn]	half past six

When do you get up?
你什么时候起床？ Nǐ shénme shíhou qǐchuáng?

I get up at 6 in the morning.
我早晨六点起床。 Wǒ zǎochen liù diǎn qǐchuáng.

① Subjective 主体	② Time 时间		③ Action 行动
you 你 [nǐ]	when 什么时候 [shénme shíhou]		get up 起床 [qǐchuáng]
		six o'clock in the morning 早晨六点 [zǎochen liù diǎn]	have breakfast 吃早饭 [chī zǎofàn]
I 我 [wǒ]	at { 在 [zài]}	half past twelve 十二点半 [shí'èr diǎn bàn]	have lunch 吃午饭 [chī wǔfàn]
			have supper 吃晚饭 [chī wǎnfàn]
he 他 [tā]		ten o'clock in the evening 晚上十点 [wǎnshang shí diǎn]	go to bed 睡觉 [shuìjiào]
Sentence Making 造句 [zàojù]	When do you go to bed? I go to bed at 10 o'clock in the evening.		你什么时候睡觉？ 我晚上十点睡觉。

Notes 注解

The general Chinese word order of a declarative sentence is "subjective + time + action". On the other hand, the general English word order is "subjective + action + time".

汉语叙述句的语序通常是"主语＋时间＋行动"。而英语叙述句的语序通常是"主语＋行动＋时间"。

Vocabulary 词语

醒来 [xǐnglái]	wake up	练习 [liànxí]	exercise
起床 [qǐchuáng]	get up	午饭 [wǔfàn]	lunch
刷牙 [shuāyá]	brush teeth	休息 [xiūxi]	rest
洗脸 [xǐliǎn]	wash face	复习 [fùxí]	review
晨练 [chénliàn]	morning exercise	课外活动 [kèwài huódòng]	outdoor activity
早餐 [zǎocān]	breakfast	回家 [huí jiā]	go back home
出门 [chūmén]	go out	晚饭 [wǎnfàn]	supper
上学 [shàngxué]	go to school	看电视 [kàn diànshì]	watch TV
上课 [shàngkè]	have class	做作业 [zuò zuòyè]	do one's homework
听讲 [tīngjiǎng]	listen to the lecturer	就寝 [jiùqǐn]	go to bed

What people did you see in the park yesterday?

您昨天在公园看见一些什么人？ Nín zuótiān zài gōngyuán kànjiàn yìxiē shénme rén?

I saw many foreign tourists in the park yesterday.

我昨天在公园看见许多外国游客。 Wǒ zuótiān zài gōngyuán kànjiàn xǔduō wàiguó yóukè.

① Subjective 主体	② Time 时间	③ Location 地点	④ Action 行动	⑤ Objective 客体	
				Amount 数量	Substance 实体
you 您 [nín]	yesterday 昨天 [zuótiān]	in the park 在公园 [zài gōngyuán]	see 看见 [kànjiàn]	{some} 一些 [yìxiē]	what people 什么人 [shénme rén]
he 他 [tā]				many 许多 [xǔduō]	foreign tourist 外国游客 [wàiguó yóukè]
we 我们 [wǒmen]	Sunday 星期日 [Xīngqīrì]	in the museum 在博物馆 [zài bówùguǎn]	meet 遇到 [yùdào]	lots of 好多 [hǎoduō]	overseas Chinese 华侨 [huáqiáo]
Sentence Making 造句 [zàojù]	What people did you meet in the park on Sunday? I met many foreign tourists in the park on Sunday.			您星期天在公园遇到一些什么人？ 我星期天在公园遇到好多外国游客。	

Notes 注解

1. In Chinese sentences temporal words or phrases are generally put before location. The sentence frame is "subjective + time + location + action + objective".

2. In Chinese "一些 [yìxiē] (some)" can be used to indicate plural conception of the nouns after it.

1. 汉语句子中通常"时间"在"地点"之前。句式为"主体＋时间＋地点＋行动＋客体"。

2. 汉语"一些 (some)"可以用来表示名词的"复数"。

Vocabulary 词语

园 [yuán]	garden; orchard	馆 [guǎn]	building; hall
花园 [huāyuán]	garden	宾馆 [bīnguǎn]	hotel
茶园 [cháyuán]	tea garden	茶馆 [cháguǎn]	teahouse
菜园 [càiyuán]	vegetable garden	咖啡馆 [kāfēiguǎn]	coffee-house
植物园 [zhíwùyuán]	botanical garden	美术馆 [měishùguǎn]	art gallery
公园 [gōngyuán]	park	博物馆 [bówùguǎn]	museum
果园 [guǒyuán]	orchard	文化馆 [wénhuàguǎn]	cultural center
桃园 [táoyuán]	peach orchard	天文馆 [tiānwénguǎn]	planetarium
苹果园 [píngguǒyuán]	apple orchard	展览馆 [zhǎnlǎnguǎn]	exhibition hall
葡萄园 [pútáoyuán]	vineyard	纪念馆 [jìniànguǎn]	memorial hall

Where is the washroom?
洗手间在哪里？ Xǐshǒujiān zài nǎli?

The washroom is on the second floor.
洗手间在二楼。 Xǐshǒujiān zài èr lóu.

① Subjective 主体	② Existing 存在	③ Location 地点
washroom 洗手间 [xǐshǒujiān] sales division 营业处 [yíngyèchù] children's wear department 童装部 [tóngzhuāngbù] manager's office 经理办公室 [jīnglǐ bàngōngshì]	be 在 [zài]	where 哪里 [nǎli] on the second floor 二楼 [èr lóu] on the third floor 三楼 [sān lóu] on the fifth floor 五楼 [wǔ lóu] on the first floor 一楼 [yī lóu]
Sentence Making 造句 [zàojù]	Where is the manager's office? The manager's office is on the first floor.	经理办公室在哪里？ 经理办公室在一楼。

Notes 注解

1. In Chinese the ordinal number is usually formed by adding the sinogram "第 [dì]" before the integer. For example, "第一 [dì-yī] (first)", "第二 [dì-èr] (second)".

2. The expression of building floor in Chinese is the same with that in American English. "第一层 [dì-yī céng]" is equivalent to "the first floor" in American English, and equivalent to "the ground floor" in British English. "第二层 [dì-èr céng]" is equivalent to "the second floor" in American English, and equivalent to "the first floor" in British English.

1. 汉语的"序数词"非常简单，即在"基数词"的前边加一个"第"。如"第一 (first)"、"第二 (second)"。

2. 汉语楼层数跟美国一致。汉语楼房"第一层"对应于美国的"the first floor"，对应于英国的"the ground floor"。汉语楼房"第二层"对应于美国的"the second floor"，对应于英国的"the first floor"。

Vocabulary 词语

处 [chù]	place; office	部 [bù]	part; department
问询处 [wènxúnchù]	enquiry office	编辑部 [biānjíbù]	editorial department
办事处 [bànshìchù]	agency	门诊部 [ménzhěnbù]	outpatient department
寄存处 [jìcúnchù]	luggage storage	住院部 [zhùyuànbù]	inpatient department
挂号处 [guàhàochù]	registration office	门市部 [ménshìbù]	sales department
售票处 [shòupiàochù]	ticket office	批发部 [pīfābù]	wholesale department
收款处 [shōukuǎnchù]	cashier's desk	修理部 [xiūlǐbù]	repair shop
登记处 [dēngjìchù]	registry office	俱乐部 [jùlèbù]	club

What are there in the sky?
天空中有什么？ Tiānkōng zhōng yǒu shénme?

There are clouds in the sky.
天空中有云。 Tiānkōng zhōng yǒu yún.

① Location 地点		② Existing 存在	③ Subjective 主体
			what 什么 [shénme]
sky 天空 [tiānkōng]	in 中 [zhōng]		cloud 云 [yún]
		there be 有 [yǒu]	star 星星 [xīngxing]
			mountain 山 [shān]
earth 地面 [dìmiàn]	on 上 [shàng]		grassland 草原 [cǎoyuán]
Sentence Making 造句 [zàojù]	What are there on the earth? There are mountains on the earth.	地面上有什么？ 地面上有山。	

Vocabulary 词语

天空 [tiānkōng]	sky	地面 [dìmiàn]	land surface
太阳 [tàiyáng]	sun	陆地 [lùdì]	land
月亮 [yuèliang]	moon	山 [shān]	mountain
星 [xīng]	star	田地 [tiándì]	field
人造卫星 [rénzào wèixīng]	man-made satellite	平原 [píngyuán]	plain
彗星 [huìxīng]	comet	草原 [cǎoyuán]	grassland
银河 [Yínhé]	Milky Way	沙漠 [shāmò]	desert
云 [yún]	cloud	湖 [hú]	lake
风 [fēng]	wind	江 [jiāng]；河 [hé]	river
雷 [léi]	thunder	海 [hǎi]	sea
雾 [wù]	fog	洋 [yáng]	ocean
雨 [yǔ]	rain	岛 [dǎo]	island
雪 [xuě]	snow	海滩 [hǎitān]	beach
冰雹 [bīngbáo]	hail; hail stone	海岸 [hǎi' àn]	seashore

What books does the library have?
图书馆有一些什么书？ Túshūguǎn yǒu yìxiē shénme shū?

The library has many books written in foreign languages.
图书馆有许多外文书。 Túshūguǎn yǒu xǔduō wàiwén shū.

①	②	③		
Organization 组织	Possessing 领有	Belongings 属物		
		Amount 数量	Attribute 属性	Substance 实体
library 图书馆 [túshūguǎn]		{some} 一些 [yìxiē]	what 什么 [shénme]	book 书 [shū] magazine
	have 有 [yǒu]		foreign(language) 外文 [wàiwén]	杂志 [zázhì] newspaper 报纸 [bàozhǐ]
book shop 书店 [shūdiàn]		many 许多 [xǔduō]	Chinese 中文 [Zhōngwén]	novel 小说 [xiǎoshuō]
Sentence Making 造句 [zàojù]	What books does the book shop have? The book shop has many novels written in Chinese.		书店有一些什么书？ 书店有许多中文小说。	

Vocabulary 词语

数学 [shùxué]	mathematics	哲学 [zhéxué]	philosophy
代数学 [dàishùxué]	algebra	历史学 [lìshǐxué]	history
几何学 [jǐhéxué]	geometry	文学 [wénxué]	literature
物理学 [wùlǐxué]	physics	古典文学 [gǔdiǎn wénxué]	classical literature
力学 [lìxué]	mechanics	现代文学 [xiàndài wénxué]	modern literature
声学 [shēngxué]	acoustics	长篇小说 [chángpiān xiǎoshuō]	novel
热学 [rèxué]	calorifics	中篇小说 [zhōngpiān xiǎoshuō]	novella
光学 [guāngxué]	optics	短篇小说 [duǎnpiān xiǎoshuō]	short story
电学 [diànxué]	electricity	传记 [zhuànjì]	biography
化学 [huàxué]	chemistry	剧本 [jùběn]	play; script
天文学 [tiānwénxué]	astronomy	诗 [shī]	poem
地理学 [dìlǐxué]	geography	散文 [sǎnwén]	prose
生物学 [shēngwùxué]	biology	寓言 [yùyán]	parable
经济学 [jīngjìxué]	economics	童话 [tónghuà]	fairy tale
法学 [fǎxué]	jurisprudence	游记 [yóujì]	travel notes

What time shall we meet?
我们什么时候见面？ Wǒmen shénme shíhou jiànmiàn?

We shall meet at half past three tomorrow afternoon.
我们明天下午三点半见面。 Wǒmen míngtiān xiàwǔ sān diǎn bàn jiànmiàn.

① Subjective 主体	② Verbal1 述谓 1 Prepositive 前辅词	Prepositive 前辅词	③ Time 时间 Period 时期	Temporal Point 时点	④ Verbal2 述谓 2 Action 行动
we 我们 [wǒmen]	shall/will 将 [jiāng]		what time 什么时候 [shénme shíhou]		meet 见面 [jiànmiàn]
you 你们 [nǐmen]	should 应该 [yīnggāi]	{at} {在 [zài]}	tomorrow afternoon 明天下午 [míngtiān xiàwǔ]	half past three 三点半 [sān diǎn bàn]	
they 他们 [tāmen]	perhaps 也许 [yěxǔ]		on Saturday evening 星期六晚上 [Xīngqīliù wǎnshang]	six o'clock 六点 [liù diǎn]	have a party 聚会 [jùhuì]
Sentence Making 造句 [zàojù]	What time will they have the party? They will have the party on Saturday evening.		他们什么时候聚会？ 他们星期六晚上聚会。		

Notes 注解

Prepositive words such as "将 [jiāng] (shall/will), 要 [yào] (would), 应该 [yīnggāi] (should), 需要 [xūyào] (need), 必须 [bìxū] (must), 能够 [nénggòu] (can), 可以 [kěyǐ] (may), 也许 [yěxǔ] (perhaps)" are generally put before certain adverbials instead of being located right before the verbal as in English.

汉语表示"情态"的"将、要、应该、需要、必须、能够、可以、也许"等辅助性词语不像英语那样一定紧接在"谓语动词"之前，而通常是位于某些"状语"之前。

Vocabulary 词语

将 [jiāng]	shall/will	见面 [jiànmiàn]	meet
应该 [yīnggāi]	should	聚会 [jùhuì]	gathering
想要 [xiǎngyào]	would	联欢 [liánhuān]	get-together
必须 [bìxū]	must	团聚 [tuánjù]	reunite
能 [néng]	can	团圆 [tuányuán]	reunion
可以 [kěyǐ]	may	合作 [hézuò]	cooperation
需要 [xūyào]	need	共事 [gòngshì]	work together
可能 [kěnéng]	might	会谈 [huìtán]	bilateral talks
或许 [huòxǔ]	perhaps	协商 [xiéshāng]	negotiate
大约 [dàyuē]	probably	结盟 [jiéméng]	form an alliance

Where will you wait for me tomorrow?
你明天在哪里等我？ Nǐ míngtiān zài nǎli děng wǒ?

I'll wait for you at the gate of the cinema tomorrow.
我明天在电影院门口等你。 Wǒ míngtiān zài diànyǐngyuàn ménkǒu děng nǐ.

| ① | ② | ③ Location 地点 | | ④ | ⑤ |
Subjective 主体	Time 时间	Prepositive 前辅词	Place 处所	Action 行动	Objective 客体
you 您 [nín]	tomorrow 明天 [míngtiān]		where 哪里 [nǎli]		me 我 [wǒ]
you 你 [nǐ]		{at} 在 [zài]	at the gate of the cinema 电影院门口 [diànyǐngyuàn ménkǒu]	wait for 等 [děng]	you 你 [nǐ]
I 我 [wǒ]	Saturday 星期六 [Xīngqīliù]		at the gate of the park 公园大门 [gōngyuán dàmén]		him 他 [tā]
Sentence Making 造句 [zàojù]	Where will you wait for him on Saturday? I'll wait for him at the main gate of the park on Saturday.			你星期六在哪里等他？ 我星期六在公园大门等他。	

Notes 注解

In Chinese the order of both time words and location words are from words expressing bigger concepts to words expressing smaller concepts, while the order in English is completely the opposite. The location order of the address on the envelope makes a sharp contrast between Chinese and English.

汉语表示"时间"和"地点"的词语，都严格地按照"从大到小"的顺序排列。汉语地点排序的"从大到小"跟英语地点排序的"从小到大"在写信封的地址上形成鲜明的对比。

二十世纪九十年代后期 [èrshí shìjì jiǔshí niándài hòuqī]	late ninetieth of the twentieth century
在二〇〇八年八月八日上午八时 [zài èr líng líng bā nián Bāyuè bā rì shàngwǔ bā shí]	at 8 a.m. in the morning on the eighth of August, 2008
在星期五下午四点十分 [zài Xīngqīwǔ xiàwǔ sì diǎn shí fēn]	at ten past four in the afternoon on Friday
在北京大学传达室的桌子上 [zài Běijīng Dàxué chuándáshì de zhuōzi shang]	on the table in the reception office of Peking University
中国吉林省长春市解放路九号 [Zhōngguó Jílín Shěng Chángchūn Shì Jiěfàng Lù jiǔ hào]	No.9 Jiefang Road, Changchun City, Jilin Province, China

IV

Shopping

购物 [gòuwù]

031. How much is this sweater? 这个毛衣多少钱？ This sweater is fifty eight yuan. 这个毛衣五十八块。

032. How much is the apple per *jin*? 苹果多少钱一斤？ It is 3 yuan per *jin*. 苹果三块钱一斤。

033. How many Chinese cabbages do you want? 你要多少白菜？
     I want five *jin* of Chinese cabbages. 我要五斤白菜。

034. How many bottles of beer do you want? 你们要几瓶啤酒？
     We want four bottles of beer. 我们要四瓶啤酒。

035. Which bag do you like? 你喜欢哪个包？ I like this bag. 我喜欢这个包。

036. Which one do you want? 你要哪一个？ I want that big one. 我要那个大的。

037. What electric appliance is bigger than a cell phone? 什么电器比手机大？
     A computer is bigger than a cell phone. 电脑比手机大。

038. What color shirt do you like? 你喜欢什么颜色的衬衫？
     I like the blue shirt. 我喜欢蓝色的衬衫。

039. What material is this skirt made of? 这个裙子是什么面料的？
     This skirt is made of silk. 这个裙子是真丝的。

040. Where are these aluminum pans produced? 这些铝锅是哪里生产的？
     These aluminum pans are produced in Shanghai. 这些铝锅是上海生产的。

How much is this sweater?
这个毛衣多少钱？ Zhège máoyī duōshao qián?

This sweater is fifty eight yuan.
这个毛衣五十八块。 Zhège máoyī wǔshíbā kuài.

① Subjective 主体		② Linking 联系	③ Relative 系体
Determiner 限定	Substance 实体		
this 这个 [zhège]	sweater 毛衣 [máoyī]		how much 多少钱 [duōshao qián]
	shirt 衬衣 [chènyī]		58 yuan 五十八块 [wǔshíbā kuài]
	skirt 裙子 [qúnzi]	be {是 [shì]}	97.50 yuan 九十七块五 [jiǔshíqī kuài wǔ]
that 那个 [nàge]	coat 外衣 [wàiyī]		276 yuan 二百七十六 [èrbǎi qīshíliù]
Sentence Making 造句 [zàojù]	How much is that overcoat? The overcoat is two hundred and seventy six yuan.		那个大衣多少钱？ 那个大衣二百七十六。

Notes 注解

In Chinese currency 人民币 (RMB) one yuan = ten *jiao* = one hundred *fen*. In oral Chinese "元 [yuán]" is called "块 [kuài]" and "角 [jiǎo]" is called "毛 [máo]". The last currency unit is always omitted.

人民币 "1 元 =10 角 =100 分"。口语称 "元" 为 "块"，称 "角" 为 "毛"。最后的货币单位经常省略。

Vocabulary 词语

衣 [yī]	clothing; clothes	钱 [qián]	money
毛衣 [máoyī]	wool clothes; sweater	货币 [huòbì]	currency
衬衣 [chènyī]	shirt	美元 [Měiyuán]	US Dollar
绒衣 [róngyī]	sweatshirt	欧元 [Ōuyuán]	Euro
外衣 [wàiyī]	coat	日元 [Rìyuán]	Yen
大衣 [dàyī]	overcoat	英镑 [Yīngbàng]	Pound Sterling
内衣 [nèiyī]	underwear	人民币 [Rénmínbì]	Renminbi (RMB)
睡衣 [shuìyī]	pajamas	元 [yuán]	yuan
浴衣 [yùyī]	bathrobe	角 [jiǎo]	*jiao*
游泳衣 [yóuyǒngyī]	swimsuit	分 [fēn]	*fen*

How much is the apple per *jin*?
苹果多少钱一斤？ Píngguǒ duōshao qián yì jīn?

It is 3 yuan per *jin*.
苹果三块钱一斤。 Píngguǒ sān kuài qián yì jīn.

①	②	③	
Subjective 主体	Linking 联系	Relative 系体	
		money 钱	weight 重量
apple 苹果 [píngguǒ]		how much 多少钱 [duōshao qián]	per *jin* 一斤 [yì jīn]
tangerine 橘子 [júzi]	be {是 [shì]}	three yuan 三块钱 [sān kuài qián]	two *jin* 二斤 [èr jīn]
melon 甜瓜 [tiánguā]		five yuan 五块钱 [wǔ kuài qián]	
chestnut 栗子 [lìzi]		ten yuan 十块钱 [shí kuài qián]	three *jin* 三斤 [sān jīn]
Sentence Making 造句 [zàojù]	How much is the melon? The melon is ten kuai for three *jin*.	甜瓜多少钱? 甜瓜十块钱三斤。	

Notes 注解

1. Conversion of Chinese unit of weights is "斤 [jīn] (*jin*)". 1 *jin* = 0.5 kilogram = 500 gram.
2. When quoting prices in Chinese, people usually quote the price as "five yuan for two *jin*", "ten yuan for five *jin*". This means psychologically the seller hopes the buyer will buy more.

1. 汉语的重量单位：1 斤 =0.5 公斤 (kg)=500 克 (g)。
2. 汉语报价时，通常把非整数"元"的价钱报成"五块钱二斤"，"十块钱五斤"。也有希望顾客多买的心理。

Vocabulary 词语

水 [shuǐ]	water	干 [gān]	dry
果 [guǒ]	fruit; result; effect	干果 [gānguǒ]	nut
水果 [shuǐguǒ]	fruit	坚果 [jiānguǒ]	nut with shell
苹果 [píngguǒ]	apple	核桃 [hétao]	walnut
芒果 [mángguǒ]	mango	栗子 [lìzi]	chestnut
桃子 [táozi]	peach	榛子 [zhēnzi]	hazelnut
橙子 [chéngzi]	orange	松子 [sōngzǐ]	pine nut
橘子 [júzi]	tangerine	瓜子 [guāzǐ]	melon seed
柚子 [yòuzi]	pomelo	杏干 [xìnggān]	dried apricot
柿子 [shìzi]	persimmon	葡萄干 [pútáogān]	raisin

How many Chinese cabbages do you want?
你要多少白菜？ Nǐ yào duōshao báicài?

I want five *jin* of Chinese cabbages.
我要五斤白菜。 Wǒ yào wǔ jīn báicài.

① Subjective 主体	② Mentality 心态	③ Objective 客体		
		Amount 数量		**Substance 实体**
you 你 [nǐ]		how many 多少 [duōshao]		Chinese cabbage 白菜 [báicài]
I 我 [wǒ]		five jin 五斤 [wǔ jīn]		spinach 菠菜 [bōcài]
he 他 [tā]	want 要 [yào]	three jin 三斤 [sān jīn]	of { }	shallot/onion 葱 [cōng]
Li Lin 李林 [Lǐ Lín]		two jin 二斤 [èr jīn]		chili 辣椒 [làjiāo]
Sentence Making 造句 [zàojù]	How many chili do you want? I want three *jin* of chili.		您要多少辣椒？ 我要三斤辣椒。	

Vocabulary 词语

菜 [cài]	vegetable; dish	瓜 [guā]	melon; gourd
蔬菜 [shūcài]	vegetable	甜瓜 [tiánguā]	melon
白菜 [báicài]	Chinese cabbage	香瓜 [xiāngguā]	muskmelon
洋白菜 [yángbáicài]	cabbage	哈密瓜 [hāmìguā]	Hami melon
包心菜 [bāoxīncài]	cabbage	西瓜 [xīguā]	water melon
菠菜 [bōcài]	spinach	菜瓜 [càiguā]	long crooked squash
芹菜 [qíncài]	celery	南瓜 [nánguā]	pumpkin
芥菜 [jiècài]	leaf mustard	笋瓜 [sǔnguā]	winter squash
韭菜 [jiǔcài]	Chinese chive	冬瓜 [dōngguā]	white gourd/winter melon
香菜 [xiāngcài]	coriander/cilantro	丝瓜 [sīguā]	towel gourd
青菜 [qīngcài]	greens	地瓜 [dìguā]	yam bean
紫菜 [zǐcài]	laver	木瓜 [mùguā]	papaya
黄花菜 [huánghuācài]	day lily	苦瓜 [kǔguā]	balsam apple/bitter melon
空心菜 [kōngxīncài]	water spinach	黄瓜 [huángguā]	cucumber

How many bottles of beer do you want?
你们要几瓶啤酒？ Nǐmen yào jǐ píng píjiǔ?

We want four bottles of beer.
我们要四瓶啤酒。Wǒmen yào sì píng píjiǔ.

① Subjective 主体	② Mentality 心态	③ Objective 客体			
		Amount 数量	Unit 单位		Substance 实体
you 你们 [nǐmen]		how many 几 [jǐ]	bottle 瓶 [píng]		beer 啤酒 [píjiǔ]
we 我们 [wǒmen]		four 四 [sì]	barrel 桶 [tǒng]		oil 油 [yóu]
he 他们 [tāmem]	want 要 [yào]	eight 八 [bā]	can 罐 [guàn]	of { }	jam 果酱 [guǒjiàng]
I 我 [wǒ]		two 两 [liǎng]	sack 袋 [dài]		flour 面粉 [miànfěn]
Sentence Making 造句 [zàojù]	How many sacks of flour do you want? I want two sacks of flour.		你要多少袋面粉？ 我要两袋面粉。		

Notes 注解

1. Nouns can be classified into countable nouns (such as person, horse and cow) and uncountable nouns (such as wine, paint and flour). There are plenty of quantifiers in Chinese. For beginners "个 [gè]" is the most useful quantifier to learn first. Expressions like "一个人 [yí gè rén] (one person), 一个马 [yí ge mǎ] (one horse), 一个牛 [yí gè niú] (one cow)" can be understood by Chinese people all over the world.

2. Both Chinese and English have borrowed quantifiers. Besides the units of weight, borrowed quantifiers mainly have containers quantifiers such as bottle, barrel and bag.

1. 名词分为 "可数名词" (人、马、牛) 和 "不可数名词" (酒、油漆、面粉)。对于 "可数名词"，汉语有非常丰富的 "量词"，初学阶段可先学会一个最有用的量词 "个"。说 "一个人、一个马、一个牛"，中国人都能听懂。

2. 汉语和英语都有 "借用量词"，除了 "重量单位" 之外，主要是 "容器单位" (瓶、桶、袋)。

Vocabulary 词语

瓶 [píng]	bottle	果汁 [guǒzhī]	juice
罐 [guàn]	jar	果酱 [guǒjiàng]	jam
盆 [pén]	basin	果酒 [guǒjiǔ]	fruit wine
碗 [wǎn]	bowl	奶油 [nǎiyóu]	cream
桶 [tǒng]	barrel/pail	奶酪 [nǎilào]	cheese
袋 [dài]	bag/sack	奶粉 [nǎifěn]	milk powder

Which bag do you like?
你喜欢哪个包？ Nǐ xǐhuan nǎge bāo?

I like this bag.
我喜欢这个包。 Wǒ xǐhuan zhège bāo.

① Subjective 主体	② Mentality 心态	③ Objective 客体	
		Determiner 限定	Substance 实物
you 你 [nǐ]	like 喜欢 [xǐhuan]	which 哪个 [nǎge]	bag 包 [bāo]
I 我 [wǒ]	find disgusting 讨厌 [tǎoyàn]	this/the 这个 [zhège]	suitcase 箱子 [xiāngzi] briefcase 公文包 [gōngwénbāo]
he 他 [tā]			
Wang Lan 王兰 [Wáng Lán]	want 要 [yào]	that/the 那个 [nàge]	safe 保险箱 [bǎoxiǎnxiāng]
Sentence Making 造句 [zàojù]	Which safe do you want? I want that safe.	你要哪个保险箱？ 我要那个保险箱。	

Notes 注解

You ought to learn how to bargain while shopping in a street market in China. A typical dialog between sellers and buyers is shown in the right table.

在"自由市场"中购物，要学会"讨价还价"。下面右边的表是"买者"和"卖者"的对话。

包 [bāo]	bag	太贵了，能便宜点儿吗？ Tài guì le, néng piányi diǎnr ma?	It's too expensive. Can you come down a bit?
提包 [tíbāo]	handbag		
挎包 [kuàbāo]	satchel	已经够便宜了。 Yǐjīng gòu piányi le.	It is cheap enough.
背包 [bēibāo]	backpack		
腰包 [yāobāo]	waist pack	你的最低价是多少？ Nǐ de zuì dī jià shì duōshao?	What is your lowest price?
钱包 [qiánbāo]	purse	您能给多少？ Nǐ néng gěi duōshao?	How much can you offer?
书包 [shūbāo]	schoolbag		
皮包 [píbāo]	leather bag	再便宜点儿，我多买一些。 Zài piányi diǎnr, wǒ duō mǎi yìxiē.	If it is cheaper, I may buy more.
公文包 [gōngwénbāo]	briefcase	好吧，给你打八折。 Hǎo ba, gěi nǐ dǎ bā zhé.	All right! Give you twenty percent discount.
旅行包 [lǚxíngbāo]	travel bag		

Which one do you want ?

你要哪一个 ？ Nǐ yào nǎ yí gè?

I want that big one.

我要那个大的。 Wǒ yào nàge dà de.

① Subjective 主体	② Mentality 心态	③ Objective 客体		
		Determiner 限定	Attribute 属性	Substance 实体
you 你 [nǐ]		which one 哪一个 [nǎ yí gè]		
I 我 [wǒ]	want 要 [yào]	this/the 这个 [zhège]	big 大 [dà]	one 的 [de]
			small 小 [xiǎo]	
			long 长 [cháng]	
he 他 [tā]		that/the 那个 [nàge]	short 短 [duǎn]	
Sentence Making 造句 [zàojù]	Which one do you want? I want the short one.		你要哪一个? 我要那个短的。	

Notes 注解

1. In Chinese "adjective + 的 [de] + noun" can be expressed as "adjective + 的 [de]" with "noun" being omitted. For example, "大的 [dà de]" indicates "大的包 [dà de bāo]".

2. Some of Chinese adjective antonyms are in pairs. The adjective antonyms in the following table are in pairs, such as big ⟷ small. Studying antonyms in pairs can be helpful for learning more vocabulary more quickly.

1. 汉语 "形容词 + 的" 而后面省略 "名词"，可代表 "形容词 + 的 + 名词"。如 "大的" 可代表 "大的包"。

2. 形容词有成对的 "反义词"。下表中的 "反义词" 成对出现。如 "大⟷小"，"big ⟷ small"。

大 [dà]	⟷ 小 [xiǎo]	big	⟷ small	好 [hǎo]	⟷ 坏 [huài]	good	⟷ bad
长 [cháng]	⟷ 短 [duǎn]	long	⟷ short	优 [yōu]	⟷ 劣 [liè]	superior	⟷ inferior
高 [gāo]	⟷ 低 [dī]	high	⟷ low	真 [zhēn]	⟷ 假 [jiǎ]	true	⟷ false
宽 [kuān]	⟷ 窄 [zhǎi]	wide	⟷ narrow	善 [shàn]	⟷ 恶 [è]	kind	⟷ vicious
深 [shēn]	⟷ 浅 [qiǎn]	deep	⟷ shallow	美 [měi]	⟷ 丑 [chǒu]	beautiful	⟷ ugly
厚 [hòu]	⟷ 薄 [báo]	thick	⟷ thin	多 [duō]	⟷ 少 [shǎo]	many	⟷ few
远 [yuǎn]	⟷ 近 [jìn]	far	⟷ near	富 [fù]	⟷ 穷 [qióng]	rich	⟷ poor
粗 [cū]	⟷ 细 [xì]	thick	⟷ thin	明 [míng]	⟷ 暗 [àn]	bright	⟷ dim
硬 [yìng]	⟷ 软 [ruǎn]	hard	⟷ soft	精 [jīng]	⟷ 笨 [bèn]	clever	⟷ stupid
浓 [nóng]	⟷ 稀 [xī]	dense	⟷ thin	强 [qiáng]	⟷ 弱 [ruò]	strong	⟷ weak

What electric appliance is bigger than a cell phone?

什么电器比手机大？ Shénme diànqì bǐ shǒujī dà?

A computer is bigger than a cell phone.

电脑比手机大。 Diànnǎo bǐ shǒujī dà.

① Subjective 主体	② Follower 伴体		③ Attribute 属性
	Prepositive 前辅词	Substance 实体	
what electric appliance 什么电器 [shénme diànqì]		cell phone 手机 [shǒujī]	big 大 [dà]
computer 电脑 [diànnǎo]	than 比 [bǐ]	telephone 电话机 [diànhuàjī]	heavy 重 [zhòng]
TV set 电视机 [diànshìjī]			
video camera 摄像机 [shèxiàngjī]		camera 照相机 [zhàoxiàngjī]	expensive 贵 [guì]
Sentence Making 造句 [zàojù]	What electric appliance is more expensive than a camera? A video camera is more expensive than a camera.		什么电器比照相机贵？ 摄像机比照相机贵。

Notes 注解

1. In Chinese adjectives haven't morphological change in "degrees". The corresponding usages of English comparative form in Chinese are: ①Sentence frame "N1 + 比 [bǐ] + N2 + A " is used to indicate comparison ②Adverb "更 [gèng] (more)" which indicates degrees is added before adjectives to express comparison. For example, "黄铜很重，银子更重 [huángtóng hěn zhòng, yínzi gèng zhòng] (Copper is heavy, silver is heavier.)" The corresponding usage of the English superlative form in Chinese is to add the adverb "最 [zuì] (most)" before adjectives. For example, "黄铜、银子、金子之中，金子最重 [huángtóng, yínzi, jīnzi zhī zhōng, jīnzi zuì zhòng] (Among copper, silver, and gold, gold is the heaviest.)"

2. In the above sentence frame, there are three substitutable columns and three phrases in each column, so the number of the generated sentence is three times three times three, which in total are twenty-seven different possible combinations. The following table shows two third of the twenty-seven sentences. These are the nine sentences starting with "电脑 [diànnǎo] (computer)" and nine sentences starting with "电视机 [diànshìjī] (TV set)". The left nine sentences staring with "摄像机 [shèxiàngjī] (video camera)" are absent.

1. 汉语没有 "级" 的词形变化。对应英语形容词 "比较级" 的用法：①如上表，用 "N1+ 比 +N2+A" 的句式；②在 "形容词" 之前加程度副词 "更"。 如 "黄铜很重，银子更重"。对应英语形容词 "最高级" 的用法，汉语在 "形容词" 之前加程度副词 "最"。如 "黄铜、银子、金子中，金子最重"。

2. 本句式中有 3 个 "可替换栏"，其 "词组" 数量分别为 3、3、3。所以本句式可生成句子数为：3×3×3=27。下表展示了 27 句的三分之二，即 "电脑" 开头的 9 句和 "电视机" 开头的 9 句，还有 "摄像机" 开头的 9 句从略。

电脑比手机大	电脑比手机重	电脑比手机贵	电视机比手机大	电视机比手机重	电视机比手机贵
电脑比电话机大	电脑比电话机重	电脑比电话机贵	电视机比电话机大	电视机比电话机重	电视机比电话机贵
电脑比照相机大	电脑比照相机重	电脑比照相机贵	电视机比照相机大	电视机比照相机重	电视机比照相机贵

What color shirt do you like?

你喜欢什么颜色的衬衫? Nǐ xǐhuan shénme yánsè de chènshān?

I like the blue shirt.

我喜欢蓝色的衬衫。 Wǒ xǐhuan lánsè de chènshān.

①	②	③		
Subjective 主体	Mentality 心态	Objective 客体		
		Attribute 属性	Postpositive 后助词	Substance 实体
you 你 [nǐ]	like 喜欢 [xǐhuan]	what color 什么颜色 [shénme yánsè]		shirt 衬衫 [chènshān]
I 我 [wǒ]		blue 蓝色 [lánsè]		skirt 裙子 [qúnzi]
he 他 [tā]	disgust 讨厌 [tǎoyàn]	red 红色 [hóngsè]	{ } 的 [de]	trousers 裤子 [kùzi]
Wang Lan 王兰 [Wáng Lán]	want 要 [yào]	yellow 黄色 [huángsè]		scarf 围巾 [wéijīn]
Sentence Making 造句 [zàojù]	What color scarf do you want? I want the red scarf.	你要什么颜色的围巾? 我要红色的围巾。		

Notes 注解

In Chinese "深 [shēn] (dark)" or "浅 [qiǎn] (light)" can be added before colors to express dark or bright colors, such as "深蓝 [shēnlán] (dark blue)", "浅蓝 [qiǎnlán] (light blue)".

汉语"深 (dark)"或"浅 (light)"加在"颜色"之前,可构成"较暗"或"较亮"的颜色,如"深蓝"、"浅蓝"。

Vocabulary 词语

心理 [xīnlǐ]	psyche; feeling	颜色 [yánsè]	color
喜欢 [xǐhuan]	like	黑 [hēi]	black
讨厌 [tǎoyàn]	be disgusted/dislike	白 [bái]	white
爱 [ài]	love	红 [hóng]	red
恨 [hèn]	hate	橙 [chéng]	orange
喜爱 [xǐ' ài]	be keen of	黄 [huáng]	yellow
珍爱 [zhēn' ài]	treasure	绿 [lǜ]	green
偏爱 [piān' ài]	favor	蓝 [lán]	blue
宠爱 [chǒng' ài]	dote on	紫 [zǐ]	purple
厌烦 [yànfán]	be sick of	棕 [zōng]	brown
愤恨 [fènhèn]	resent	灰 [huī]	grey

What material is this skirt made of?
这个裙子是什么面料的？ Zhège qúnzi shì shénme miànliào de?

This skirt is made of silk.
这个裙子是真丝的。 Zhège qúnzi shì zhēnsī de.

① Subjective 主体		② Linking 联系	③ Relative 系体		
Determiner 限定	Substance 实物		Material 材料	Action 行动	Postpositive 后助词
this 这个 [zhège]	skirt 裙子 [qúnzi]		what material 什么面料 [shénme miànliào]		
	cheongsam 旗袍 [qípáo]	be 是 [shì]	silk 真丝 [zhēnsī]	make {做 [zuò]}	{ } 的 [de]
that 那个 [nàge]	suit 西服 [xīfú]		woolen fabric 毛料 [máoliào]		
Sentence Making 造句 [zàojù]	What material is that suit made of? The suit is made of woolen fabric.		那个西服是什么面料的？ 那个西服是毛料的。		

Notes 注解

Most sinograms contain a radical, which is often located on the left half of the sinogram, and indicates the semantic categories of the sinograms. For example, "纟" is the left part of "丝 [sī] (silk)". It is called "丝字旁 [sīzìpáng]". All sinograms with the radical "纟"are related to the meaning of "silk" or "weaving".
汉语绝大多数"字"的半边是表示"意义类别"的"字基（部首）"(radical)。如"纟"是"丝"字的左半边，叫做"丝字旁"。凡是有"纟(丝字旁)"的字都跟"丝绸"和"纺织"的意思有关。

Vocabulary 词语

丝 [sī]	silk	线 [xiàn]	thread
绸子 [chóuzi]	silk fabric	棉线 [miánxiàn]	cotton thread
缎子 [duànzi]	satin	丝线 [sīxiàn]	silk thread
纺 [fǎng]	spin	绳 [shéng]	rope
织 [zhī]	weave	麻绳 [máshéng]	hemp rope
纺织品 [fǎngzhīpǐn]	textile; fabric	棕绳 [zōngshéng]	coir rope (from the coconut husk)
纱 [shā]	yarn	缆 [lǎn]	mooring rope; cable
纺纱 [fǎngshā]	spinning	电缆 [diànlǎn]	electric cable
编织 [biānzhī]	knit	绒 [róng]	velvet
织布 [zhībù]	weave cloth	缝 [féng]	sew

Where are these aluminum pans produced?
这些铝锅是哪里生产的？ Zhèxiē lǚguō shì nǎlǐ shēngchǎn de?

These aluminum pans are produced in Shanghai.
这些铝锅是上海生产的。 Zhèxiē lǚguō shì Shànghǎi shēngchǎn de.

①		②	③		
Subjective 主体		Linking 联系	Relative 系体		
Determiner 限定	Substance 实体		Location 地点	Action 行动	Postpositive 后助词
these 这些 [zhèxiē]	aluminum pan 铝锅 [lǚguō]		where 哪里 [nǎlǐ]	produce 生产 [shēngchǎn]	
	steel saw 钢锯 [gāngjù]		Shanghai 上海 [Shànghǎi]	make 制造 [zhìzào]	
this 这个 [zhège]		be(is) 是 [shì]			{ } 的 [de]
	shovel 铁锹 [tiěqiāo]		Guangzhou 广州 [Guǎngzhōu]	make 造 [zào]	
that/the 那个 [nàge]	gold necklace 金项链 [jīnxiàngliàn]		Hong Kong 香港 [Xiānggǎng]	make 做 [zuò]	
Sentence Making 造句 [zàojù]	Where is the gold necklace made? The gold necklace is made in Hong Kong.		这个金项链是哪里做的? 这个金项链是香港做的。		

Notes 注解

The radical "钅" is the changed form of "金 [jīn] (gold)." It is called "金字旁 [jīnzìpáng]". All sinograms with the radical "钅" have the meaning related to "metal" or "metal products".

字基(部首) "钅" 是 "金" 的变体，叫 "金字旁"。凡是 "钅(金字旁)" 的字都跟 "金属及其制品" 的意思有关。

Vocabulary 词语

金 [jīn]	gold	锅 [guō]	pot
银 [yín]	silver	铲 [chǎn]	spade
铜 [tóng]	copper	锹 [qiāo]	shovel
铁 [tiě]	iron	锤 [chuí]	hammer
钢 [gāng]	steel	锯 [jù]	saw
铝 [lǚ]	aluminum	钳 [qián]	pliers, pincers
钙 [gài]	calcium	钻 [zuàn]	drill
钠 [nà]	natrium/sodium	锉 [cuò]	file
钾 [jiǎ]	potassium	键 [jiàn]	key
铅 [qiān]	plumbum/lead	锁 [suǒ]	lock
锌 [xīn]	zinc	链 [liàn]	chain

V

Eating and Drinking
吃喝 [chī hē]

041. What restaurants are there around here? 这周围有什么饭馆？

There is a western restaurant nearby. 附近有一个西餐厅。

042. How many are there in your party? 你们一共有几位？

There are eight people in our party. 我们一共有八个人。

043. How long do we need to wait? 我们要等多久？

You have to wait for ten minutes. 您得等十分钟。

044. What specialties do you have? 你们有什么特色菜？

We have fish-flavored shredded pork. 我们有鱼香肉丝。

045. What would you like to eat? 你想吃什么？

I'd like to eat Beijing Roast Duck. 我想吃北京烤鸭。

046. How dose it taste? 味道怎么样？　　　　　　　　　　　　It is a little salty. 味道有点儿咸。

047. What kind of alcohol do you have? 你们有什么酒？　　　　We have Moutai. 我们有茅台。

048. What would you like to drink? 你想喝什么？　　　　　　I'd like to drink beer. 我想喝啤酒。

049. What do you like to eat in the summer? 你夏天喜欢吃什么？

I like to eat ice cream in the summer. 我夏天喜欢吃冰淇淋。

050. What does Li Hua cook for her grandpa with a small pot in the kitchen every day? 李华每天在厨房用小锅给爷爷煮什么？

Li Hua boils milk for her grandpa with a small pot in the kitchen every day.

李华每天在厨房用小锅给爷爷煮牛奶。

What restaurants are there around here?
这周围有什么饭馆？ Zhè zhōuwéi yǒu shénme fànguǎn?

There is a western restaurant nearby.
附近有一个西餐厅。 Fùjìn yǒu yí ge xīcāntīng.

① Location 地点	② Existing 存在	③ Subjective 主体	
		Amount 数量	Place 处所
around here 这周围 [zhè zhōuwéi] nearby 这附近 [zhè fùjìn] in front 前边 [qiánbian] on the left 左边 [zuǒbian]	there be 有 [yǒu]	{a} {一个 [yí gè]}	what restaurant 什么饭馆 [shénme fànguǎn] western restaurant 西餐厅 [xīcāntīng] fast food restaurant 快餐店 [kuàicāndiàn] snack bar 小吃店 [xiǎochīdiàn]
Sentence Making 造句 [zàojù]	What restaurants are there nearby? There is a Sichuan restaurant on the left.	这附近有什么饭馆？ 左边有一个四川饭馆。	

Vocabulary 词语

近 [jìn]	near; close	饭 [fàn]; 餐 [cān]	meal
附近 [fùjìn]	nearby	早饭 [zǎofàn]; 早餐 [zǎocān]	breakfast
四周 [sìzhōu]	all around	午饭 [wǔfàn]; 午餐 [wǔcān]	lunch
边 [biān]	side; edge	晚饭 [wǎnfàn]; 晚餐 [wǎncān]	supper
前边 [qiánbian]	in front	便饭 [biànfàn]	a simple meal
后边 [hòubian]	at the back; behind	米饭 [mǐfàn]	rice
里边 [lǐbian]	inside	聚餐 [jùcān]; 会餐 [huìcān]	banquet
外边 [wàibian]	outside	中餐 [zhōngcān]	Chinese food
上边 [shàngbian]	above; over	西餐 [xīcān]	Western-style food
下边 [xiàbian]	down; below	快餐 [kuàicān]	fast food; snack
左边 [zuǒbian]	left	自助餐 [zìzhùcān]	buffet
右边 [yòubian]	right	饭馆 [fànguǎn]	restaurant
路边 [lùbiān]	side of the road	餐厅 [cāntīng]	dining hall
周边 [zhōubiān]	surrounding	宴会厅 [yànhuìtīng]	banquet hall

How many are there in your party?
你们一共有几位？ Nǐmen yígòng yǒu jǐ wèi?

There are eight people in our party.
我们一共有八个人。Wǒmen yígòng yǒu bā ge rén.

① Location 地点	② Existing 存在	③ Subjective 主体
in your party 你们一共 [nǐmen yígòng]		how many 几位 [jǐ wèi]
		eight people 八个人 [bā ge rén]
	there be (is/are) 有 [yǒu]	ten people 十个人 [shí ge rén]
in our party 我们一共 [wǒmen yígòng]		twelve people 十二个人 [shí' èr ge rén]
Sentence Making 造句 [zàojù]	How many are there in your party? There are 12 people in our party.	你们一共有几位？ 我们一共有十二个人。

Notes 注解

1. "们 [men]" expresses a plural conception when it is added after nouns of personal reference or pronouns. For instance, "工人 [gōngrén] (worker) →工人们 [gōngrénmen] (workers)" "他 [tā] (he) → 他们 [tāmen] (they)".

2. "们 [men]" cannot be added after nouns without personal reference. That is to say:
   "桌子 [zhuōzi] (table) → * 桌子们 [zhuōzimen] (tables)" can not be reasoned out by analogy.

3. If there are exact numbers and approximate numbers before a noun of personal reference which has shown the plural conception, "们 [men]" shouldn't be added before that noun to indicate plural conception. But the followings cannot be reasoned out by analogy: "三个工人 [sān ge gōngrén] (three workers)" → * "三个工人们 [sān ge gōngrénmen]" "许多工人 [xǔduō gōngrén] (many workers)" → * 许多工人们 [xǔduō gōngrénmen]".

1. 汉语的"们"加在"指人名词"和"人称代词"之后表示"复数"。例如："工人(worker)→工人们(workers)"；"学生(student) → 学生们(students)"；"我（I）→ 我们(we)"；"他(he) → 他们(they)"。

2. 不指人的名词复数不能加"们"。不能类推"桌子 (table) → * 桌子们 (tables)"。

3. 汉语指人名词的前边已用"确定的数量词"或"概数词"指明了"复数"时，该名词也不能加"们"。例如：不能类推"三个工人(three workers) → * 三个工人们"；"许多工人(many workers) → * 许多工人们"。

Vocabulary 词语

厨师 [chúshī]	chef	服务员 [fúwùyuán]	attendant
教师 [jiàoshī]; 老师 [lǎoshī]	teacher	职员 [zhíyuán]	staff
律师 [lǜshī]	lawyer	售货员 [shòuhuòyuán]	shop assistant
工程师 [gōngchéngshī]	engineer	售票员 [shòupiàoyuán]	ticket seller

043 How long do we need to wait?
我们要等多久？ Wǒmen yào děng duōjiǔ?

You have to wait for ten minutes.
您得等十分钟 。 Nín děi děng shí fēnzhōng.

	①	② Verbal 述谓		③
	Subjective 主体	Prepositive 前辅词	Action 行动	Duration 时量
	we 我们 [wǒmen]	need to 要 [yào]	wait 等 [děng]	how long 多久 [duōjiǔ]
	I 我 [wǒ]			for ten minutes 十分钟 [shí fēnzhōng]
	you 您 [nín]	have to 得 [děi]	stay 停留 [tíngliú]	for a quarter of an hour 一刻钟 [yí kèzhōng]
	he 他 [tā]			for half an hour 半小时 [bàn xiǎoshí]
Sentence Making 造句 [zàojù]	How long does he need to stay? He has to stay for a quarter of an hour.		他要等多久？ 他得等一刻钟。	

Notes 注解

1. The radical "饣" is the changed form of "食 [shí] (food)". It is called "食字旁 [shízìpáng]". Sinograms with radical "饣" all have meanings of "food" or "eating and drinking".

2. The radical "火 (火字旁 [huǒzìpáng])" and "灬 (火字底 [huǒzìdǐ])" are changed forms of "火 [huǒ] (fire)". Sinograms with radical "火" and "灬" all have meanings of "火 [huǒ] (fire)". Most sinograms in terms of cooking or culinary art have radical "火" or "灬" for the reason that people use fire to cook food.

1. 字基(部首) "饣" 是 "食" 的变体，叫 "食字旁"。凡是 "饣(食字旁)" 的字都有 "食品或饮食" 的意思。

2. 字基(部首) "火(火字旁)" 和 "灬 (火字底)" 都是 "火" 的变体。凡是 "火 (火字旁)" 和 "灬(火字底)" 的字都有 "火" 的意思。人们烧饭和炒菜都要用 "火"，所以有关 "烹饪" 方法的字，大多有字基(部首) "火(火字旁)" 和 "灬(火字底)"。

Vocabulary 词语

饿 [è]	hungry	炒 [chǎo]	stir-fry
饱 [bǎo]	full	炸 [zhá]	deep fry
饼 [bǐng]	cake, pastry	烤 [kǎo]	grill
饺子 [jiǎozi]	Chinese dumpling	烙 [lào]	bake in a pan
馍 [mó]	steamed bun	煮 [zhǔ]	boil
馒头 [mántou]	steamed bun	煎 [jiān]	fry
饮 [yǐn]	drink	烹 [pēng]	cook
饮料 [yǐnliào]	soft drink	蒸 [zhēng]	steam

What specialties do you have?
你们有什么特色菜？ Nǐmen yǒu shéme tèsè cài?

We have fish-flavored shredded pork.
我们有鱼香肉丝。 Wǒmen yǒu yúxiāng ròusī.

①	②	③
Subjective 主体	Possessing 领有	Belongings 属物
you 你们 [nǐmen]		what specialties 什么特色菜 [shéme tèsè cài]
		fish-flavored shredded pork 鱼香肉丝 [yúxiāng ròusī]
we 我们 [wǒmen]	have 有 [yǒu]	fried diced chicken with cashew nuts 腰果鸡丁 [yāoguǒ jīdīng]
		shredded beef fried on an iron plate 铁板牛柳 [tiěbǎn niúliǔ]
they 他们 [tāmen]		diced chicken with hot peppers 宫爆鸡丁 [gōngbào jīdīng]
Sentence Making 造句 [zàojù]	What specialties do you have? We have diced chicken with hot peppers.	你们有什么特色菜？ 我们有宫爆鸡丁。

Vocabulary 词语

菜 [cài]	dishes; vegetables
北京烤鸭 [Běijīng kǎoyā]	Beijing Roast Duck
糖醋鲤鱼 [tángcù lǐyú]	sweet and sour fish
西红柿炒鸡蛋 [xīhóngshì chǎo jīdàn]	fried eggs with tomato
鱼香肉丝 [yúxiāng ròusī]	fish-flavored shredded pork
腰果鸡丁 [yāoguǒ jīdīng]	fried diced chicken with cashew nuts
宫爆鸡丁 [gōngbào jīdīng]	diced chicken in spicy sauce
辣子鸡丁 [làzi jīdīng]	diced chicken with green pepper
铁板牛柳 [tiěbǎn niúliǔ]	shredded beef fried on an iron plate
鱼香茄子 [yúxiāng qiézi]	eggplant in spicy sauce
京酱肉丝 [jīngjiàng ròusī]	pork in sauce over scallions
烤乳猪 [kǎorǔzhū]	roasted suckling pig
焖牛肉 [mènniúròu]	braised beef
家常豆腐 [jiācháng dòufu]	home-cooked bean curd/tofu
红烧排骨 [hóngshāo páigǔ]	braised ribs in brown sauce
豆腐海带汤 [dòufu hǎidàitāng]	bean curd and kelp soup
涮羊肉 [shuànyángròu]	mutton hot pot; instant-boiled mutton
什锦火锅 [shíjǐn huǒguō]	assorted hot pot
莲子羹 [liánzǐgēng]	lotus seeds porridge
八宝饭 [bābǎofàn]	eight-treasure rice pudding

What would you like to eat?
你想吃什么? Nǐ xiǎng chī shénme?

I'd like to eat Beijing Roast Duck.
我想吃北京烤鸭。 Wǒ xiǎng chī Běijīng kǎoyā.

① Subjective 主体	② Verbal 述谓		③ Objective 客体
	Mentality 心态	Action 行动	
you 你 [nǐ]	would like to 想 [xiǎng]		what 什么 [shénme]
			Beijing Roast Duck 北京烤鸭 [Běijīng kǎoyā]
you 您 [nín]		eat 吃 [chī]	sweet and sour fish 糖醋鲤鱼 [tángcù lǐyú]
I 我 [wǒ]	want to 要 [yào]		steamed stuffed bun 包子 [bāozi]
Sentence Making 造句 [zàojù]	What do you want to eat? I want to eat steamed stuffed bun.		你要吃什么? 我要吃包子。

Notes 注解

The radical "口" is the changed form of "口 [kǒu] (mouth)." It is called "口字旁 [kǒuzìpáng]". Sinograms with the radical "口" all have meanings of mouth or the action of the mouth (eat, drink, suck, shout, sing, etc.)".

字基(部首)"口"是"口"的变体,叫"口字旁"。有字基(部首)"口"的字都跟"口(嘴、喉)和口的动作(吃、喝、吸、唱)"的意思有关。

Vocabulary 词语

吃 [chī]	eat	呼 [hū]	exhale
咬 [yǎo]	bite	吸 [xī]	breathe in; suck
啃 [kěn]	gnaw	呼吸 [hūxī]	breath
叼 [diāo]	hold in mouth	吹 [chuī]	blow
嚼 [jiáo]	chew	叫 [jiào]	call
咽 [yàn]	swallow	喊 [hǎn]	shout
喝 [hē]	drink	叹 [tàn]	sigh
吐 [tù]	vomit; spit	吵 [chǎo]	quarrel; noisy
唾 [tuò]	spit; spittle	唱 [chàng]	sing
喷 [pēn]	spray	哼 [hēng]	groan; moan

How dose it taste?
味道怎么样？ Wèidào zěnmeyàng?

It is a little salty.
味道有点儿咸。Wèidào yǒudiǎnr xián.

① Subjective 主体	② Linking 联系	③ Relative 系体
taste 味道 [wèidào]	be { }	how (what is it like) 怎么样 [zěnmeyàng] a little salty 有点儿咸 [yǒudiǎnr xián] OK 还行 [hái xíng] delicious 好极了 [hǎojí le] too spicy 太辣了 [tài là le]
Sentence Making 造句 [zàojù]	How does it taste? It is delicious.	味道怎么样？ 味道好极了。

Notes   注解

1. The sinogram "好 [hǎo] (good)" added before verbs expresses the meaning of "满意 [mǎnyì] (to be satisfied with)" or "易于 [yìyú] (to be easy to)".

2. The sinogram "难 [nán] (difficult)" added before a verb expresses the meaning of "不满 [bùmǎn] (to be not satisfied with)" or "难于 [nányú] (to be difficult to)". Words in the following left and right tables form antonyms in pairs.

1. "好" 字加在动词之前可表示 "满意" 或 "易于" 的意思。

2. "难" 字加在动词之前可表示 "不满" 或 "难于" 的意思，下列的左表和右表形成两组相对的 "反义词"。

Vocabulary   词语

好吃 [hǎochī]	good to eat; delicious	难吃 [nánchī]	taste bad
好喝 [hǎohē]	good to drink	难喝 [nánhē]	unpleasant to drink
好闻 [hǎowén]	pleasant to smell	难闻 [nánwén]	unpleasant to smell
好看 [hǎokàn]	good looking; pretty	难看 [nánkàn]	unsightily; ugly
好听 [hǎotīng]	pleasant to hear	难听 [nántīng]	unpleasant to hear; strident
好受 [hǎoshòu]	feel better	难受 [nánshòu]	feel ill; feel sad
好学 [hǎoxué]	easy to learn	难学 [nánxué]	difficult to learn
好记 [hǎojì]	easy to memorize	难记 [nánjì]	difficult to memorize
好办 [hǎobàn]	easy to handle	难办 [nánbàn]	difficult to handle

What kind of alcohol do you have?
你们有什么酒？ Nǐmen yǒu shéme jiǔ?

We have Moutai.
我们有茅台。 Wǒmen yǒu Máotái.

① Subjective 主体	② Possessing 领有	③ Belongings 属物
you 你们 [nǐmen] we 我们 [wǒmen] they 他们 [tāmen] that restaurant 那个饭店 [nàge fàndiàn]	have 有 [yǒu]	what alcohol 什么酒 [shéme jiǔ] Moutai 茅台 [Máotái] whiskey 威士忌 [wēishìjì] brandy 白兰地 [báilándì] French wine 法国葡萄酒 [Fǎguó pútaojiǔ]
Sentence Making 造句 [zàojù]	What kinds of alcohol do you have? We have French wine.	你们有什么酒？ 我们有法国葡萄酒。

Vocabulary 词语

酒 [jiǔ]	alcoholic drink; liquor	饮料 [yǐnliào]	beverages; drink
白酒 [báijiǔ]	Chinese spirits; liquor	汽水 [qìshuǐ]	soft drink
啤酒 [píjiǔ]	beer	矿泉水 [kuàngquánshuǐ]	mineral water
黄酒 [huángjiǔ]	yellow rice wine	橙汁 [chéngzhī]	orange juice
白葡萄酒 [bái pútaojiǔ]	white wine	苹果汁 [píngguǒzhī]	apple juice
红葡萄酒 [hóng pútaojiǔ]	red wine	柠檬汁 [níngméngzhī]	lemon juice
香槟酒 [xiāngbīnjiǔ]	champagne	番茄汁 [fānqiézhī]	tomato juice
鸡尾酒 [jīwěijiǔ]	cocktail	鲜牛奶 [xiānniúnǎi]	fresh milk
苹果酒 [píngguǒjiǔ]	cider	酸奶 [suānnǎi]	yogurt
杜松子酒 [dùsōngzǐjiǔ]	gin	奶茶 [nǎichá]	tea with milk
马提尼酒 [mǎtíníjiǔ]	martini	可口可乐 [kěkǒukělè]	Coca-Cola
白兰地 [báilándì]	brandy	咖啡 [kāfēi]	coffee
伏特加 [fútèjiā]	vodka	红茶 [hóngchá]	black tea
威士忌 [wēishìjì]	whisky	绿茶 [lùchá]	green tea

What would you like to drink?
你想喝什么？ Nǐ xiǎng hē shénme?

I'd like to drink beer.
我想喝啤酒。 Wǒ xiǎng hē píjiǔ.

①	②		③
	Verbal 述谓		
Subjective 主体	Mentality 心态	Action 行动	Objective 客体
you 你 [nǐ]	would like to 想 [xiǎng]		what 什么 [shénme]
I 我 [wǒ]		drink 喝 [hē]	beer 啤酒 [píjiǔ] orange juice 橙汁 [chéngzhī]
you 您 [nín]	want to 要 [yào]		green tea 绿茶 [lǜchá]
Sentence Making 造句 [zàojù]	What do you want to drink? I want to drink green tea.		你要喝什么？ 我要喝绿茶。

Notes 注解

The radical "氵" is the changed form of "水 [shuǐ] (water)". It is called "三点水 [sāndiǎoshuǐ]". Sinograms with the radical "氵" have meanings related to water or liquid.

字基(部首) "氵" 是 "水" 的变体，叫做 "三点水"。凡是有字基(部首) "氵" 的字都跟 "水和液体" 的意思有关。

Vocabulary 词语

水 [shuǐ]	water	液 [yè]	liquid; fluid
汗 [hàn]	sweat	液体 [yètǐ]	liquid
泪 [lèi]	tear	汁 [zhī]	juice
浪 [làng]	wave	油 [yóu]	oil
流 [liú]	flow	酒 [jiǔ]	wine
沟 [gōu]	ditch; channel	汤 [tāng]	soup
池 [chí]	pool	泥 [ní]	mud
湖 [hú]	lake	潮 [cháo]	humid
江 [jiāng]; 河 [hé]	river	湿 [shī]	wet
海 [hǎi]	sea	浮 [fú]	float
洋 [yáng]	ocean	游 [yóu]	swim

What do you like to eat in the summer?
你夏天喜欢吃什么？ Nǐ xiàtiān xǐhuan chī shénme?

I like to eat ice cream in the summer.
我夏天喜欢吃冰淇淋。 Wǒ xiàtiān xǐhuan chī bīngqílín.

① Subjective 主体	② Time 时间	③ Verbal 述谓		④ Objective 客体
		Mentality 心态	Action 行动	
you 你 [nǐ]		would like to 喜欢 [xǐhuan]		what 什么 [shénme]
	summer 夏天 [xiàtiān]		eat 吃 [chī]	ice cream 冰淇淋 [bīngqílín]
				popsicle 冰棍儿 [bīnggùnr]
I 我 [wǒ]		want to 想 [xiǎng]		snow cone 刨冰 [bàobīng]
Sentence Making 造句 [zàojù]	What do you like to eat in the summer? I like to eat snow cones in the summer.		你夏天喜欢吃什么？ 我夏天喜欢吃刨冰。	

Notes 注解

The radical "冫" is the left part of "冷 [lěng] (cold)". It is called "冷字旁 [lěngzìpáng]". Most sinograms with the radical "冫" have meanings related to "cold". The two dots at the bottom part of "冬 [dōng] (winter)" and "寒 [hán] (cold)" are also the changed form of "冫" and also have meanings related to "cold".

字基(部首) "冫" 是 "冷" 的左偏旁，叫做 "冷字旁"。有字基(部首) "冫(冷字旁)" 的字大多数跟 "冷" 的意思有关。"冬" 和 "寒" 底部的 "两点" 也是 "冫" 的变体，也有 "冷" 的意思。

Vocabulary 词语

春 [chūn]	spring	冬 [dōng]	winter
暖 [nuǎn]	warm; warm up	寒 [hán]	frigid; cold
温暖 [wēnnuǎn]	warm	冷 [lěng]	cold
夏 [xià]	summer	凉 [liáng]	cool
热 [rè]	hot; heat; heat up	冻 [dòng]	freeze; freezing
炎热 [yánrè]	burning hot	冰 [bīng]	ice; icy
秋 [qiū]	autumn	凌 [líng]	icicle
爽 [shuǎng]	clear; feel well	凄 [qī]	chilly; frigid
清爽 [qīngshuǎng]	clear and fresh	凝 [níng]	congeal; freeze

What does Li Hua cook for her grandpa with a small pot in the kitchen every day?
李华每天在厨房用小锅给爷爷煮什么？ Lǐ Huá měi tiān zài chúfáng yòng xiǎo guō gěi yéye zhǔ shénme?

Li Hua boils milk for her grandpa with a small pot in the kitchen every day.
李华每天在厨房用小锅给爷爷煮牛奶。 Lǐ Huá měi tiān zài chúfáng yòng xiǎo guō gěi yéye zhǔ niúnǎi.

① Subjective 主体	② Time 时间	③ Location 地点	④ Follower 伴体	⑤ Beneficiary 涉体	⑥ Action 行动	⑦ Objective 客体
Li Hua 李华 [Lǐ Huá]	every day 每天 [měi tiān]		with a small pot 用小锅 [yòng xiǎo guō]	for Grandpa 给爷爷 [gěi yéye]		what 什么 [shénme]
		in the kitchen 在厨房 [zài chúfáng]			boil 煮 [zhǔ]	milk 牛奶 [niúnǎi]
Liu Mei 刘梅 [Liú Méi]	after work 下班后 [xiàbān hòu]		with a clay pot 用砂锅 [yòng shāguō]	for Grandma 给奶奶 [gěi nǎinai]		egg 鸡蛋 [jīdàn]

Sentence Making 造句 [zàojù]	What did Liu Mei boil for her grandma with a clay pot in the kitchen after work? 刘梅下班后在厨房用砂锅给奶奶煮什么？ Liu Mei boiled eggs for her grandma with a clay pot in the kitchen after work. 刘梅下班后在厨房用砂锅给奶奶煮鸡蛋。

Notes 注解

A basic Chinese sentence is a kind of sentence without "chunk movement according to context." A basic sentence frame is constituted by 7±2 semantic roles. The order of the semantic roles is fixed. The sentence "李华每天在厨房用小锅给爷爷煮牛奶" is constituted by seven semantic roles. If two more semantic roles, "causative" and "measure" are added, then a complete basic sentence with nine semantic roles are constituted as the sentence in the following table. In an incomplete sentence, the order of the semantic roles is still fixed. It is useful for learners to memorize the order of a Chinese sentence as: "① subjective, ②causative, ③time, ④location, ⑤follower, ⑥beneficiary, ⑦verbal, ⑧dative, ⑨objective".

汉语"基础句"是没有"语境移位"的句子。一个基础句由7±2个"语义角色"组成，语序十分固定。上表中的"李华每天在厨房用小锅给爷爷煮牛奶"由7个"语义角色"组成。如增加2个语义角色"原由"和"度量"，就可组成下表有9个"语义角色"的完整的基础句。不完整的基础句中，语义角色之间的顺序仍是固定的。学习者记住"①主体，②原由，③时间，④地点，⑤伴体，⑥涉体，⑦述谓，⑧邻体，⑨客体"的汉语顺序是很有用的。

①	②	③	④	⑤	⑥	⑦	⑧	⑨
subjective 主体 [zhǔtǐ]	causative 原由 [yuányóu]	time 时间 [shíjiān]	location 地点 [dìdiǎn]	follower 伴体 [bàntǐ]	beneficiary 涉体 [shètǐ]	verbal 述谓 [shùwèi]	dative 邻体 [líntǐ] measure 度量 [dùliàng]	objective 客体 [kè-tǐ] relative 系体 [xìtǐ]
Li Hua 李华 [Lǐ Huá]	according to the order 按吩咐 [àn fēnfù]	every day 每天 [měi tiān]	in the kitchen 在厨房 [zài chúfáng]	with a small pot 用小锅 [yòng xiǎo guō]	for her grandpa 给爷爷 [gěi yéye]	boil 煮 [zhǔ]	three time 三次 [sān cì]	milk 牛奶 [niúnǎi]

②According to the order, ①Li Hua ⑦boil ⑨milk ⑧three times ⑥for her grandpa ⑤with a small pot ④in the kitchen ③every day.

Accommodation

住宿 [zhùsù]

051. Where are you staying? 你住在哪里？ I am staying in a hotel. 我住在宾馆里。

052. What kind of room would you like to book? 您想订什么房间？
I'd like to book a standard room. 我想订一个标准间。

053. When are you going to check in? 您打算什么时候入住？
I'm going to check in on May 7. 我打算五月七号入住。

054. How long did he sleep last Friday? 他上星期五睡了多长时间？
He slept for 4 hours last Friday. 他上星期五睡了四个小时。

055. What is there in the room? 房间里有什么？
There is an air conditioner in the room. 房间里有空调。

056. Which direction do those windows face? 那些窗子朝哪个方向？
Those windows face toward the south. 那些窗子朝南。

057. By whom was your room card lost? 你们的房卡被谁弄丢了？
Our room card was lost by my son. 我们的房卡被我儿子弄丢了。

058. How do you want your hair to be cut? 你想把头发剪成什么样？
I'd like to have my hair cut shorter. 我想把头发剪短点儿。

059. What trees are there in this residential quarter? 这个住宅区里有什么树？
There are many pines in this residential quarter. 这个住宅区里有很多松树。

060. What flowers are there in this flower bed? 这个花坛里有什么花？
There are many red roses in this flower bed. 这个花坛里有很多红玫瑰。

Where are you staying?
你住在哪里？ Nǐ zhù zài nǎli?

I am staying in a hotel.
我住在宾馆里。 Wǒ zhù zài bīnguǎn li.

① Subjective 主体	② State 状态	③ Location 地点		
		Prepositive 前辅词	Place 处所	Postpositive 后助词
you 你 [nǐ]			where 哪里 [nǎli]	
I 我 [wǒ]	stay 住 [zhù]	{at} 在 [zài]	hotel 宾馆 [bīnguǎn]	in {里 [li]}
he 他 [tā]			Chaoyang Residential Quarter 朝阳小区 [cháoyáng xiǎoqū]	
Li Ming 李明 [Lǐ Mǐng]			No.18 Xueyuan Road 学院路 18 号 [xuéyuàn lù shíbā hào]	
Sentence Making 造句 [zàojù]	Where does Li Ming live? He lives at No.18, Xueyuan Road.		李明住在哪里？ 他住在学院路 18 号。	

Notes 注解

In Chinese "在 [zài] + N + 里 [li]" is equivalent to "in + N" in English, and "在 [zài]" or "里 [li]" is sometimes absent.

英语 "in+N" 对应于汉语 "在+N+里"。有时汉语可以省略 "在" 或 "里"。

Vocabulary 词语

宾馆 [bīnguǎn]；饭店 [fàndiàn]	hotel	市 [shì]	city
友谊宾馆 [Yǒuyí Bīnguǎn]	Friendship Hotel	区 [qū]	district; region; area
北京饭店 [Běijīng Fàndiàn]	Beijing Hotel	小区 [xiǎoqū]	housing area
国际饭店 [Guójì Fàndiàn]	International Hotel	住宅区 [zhùzhái qū]	residential quarter
旅馆 [lǚguǎn]；旅店 [lǚdiàn]	hotel	新区 [xīnqū]	new area
公寓 [gōngyù]	apartment	郊区 [jiāoqū]	suburb
宿舍 [sùshè]	dormitory	街 [jiē]	street
学生宿舍 [xuésheng sùshè]	student dormitory	路 [lù]	road
房 [fáng]	house	院 [yuàn]	courtyard
出租房 [chūzū fáng]	house for rent	门牌 [ménpái]	address sign
楼 [lóu]	building	号 [hào]	number

What kind of room would you like to book?

您想订什么房间？ Nín xiǎng dìng shénme fángjiān?

I'd like to book a standard room.

我想订一个标准间。 Wǒ xiǎng dìng yí gè biāozhǔnjiān.

①	②		③	
Subjective 主体	Verbal 述谓		Objective 客体	
	Mentality 心态	Action 行动		
you (with respect) 您 [nín]	would like to 想 [xiǎng]		what room 什么房间 [shénme fángjiān]	
		book 订 [dìng]	a 一个 [yí gè]	standard room 标准间 [biāozhǔnjiān]
				room on an upper floor 楼层高的房间 [lóucéng gāo de fángjiān]
I 我 [wǒ]	want to 要 [yào]		three 三个 [sān gè]	single room 单人间 [dānrénjiān]
Sentence Making 造句 [zàojù]	What kind of room would you like to book? I want to book three single rooms.		你想订什么房间？ 我想订三个单人间。	

Notes 注解

The general Chinese word order of a declarative sentence is "subjective + time + action." On the other hand, the general English word order of a declarative sentence is "subjective + action + time".

汉语叙述句的语序通常是"主体＋时间＋行动"。而英语叙述句的语序通常是"主体＋行动＋时间"。

Vocabulary 词语

前台 [qiántái]	reception desk	单人间 [dānrénjiān]	single room
登记簿 [dēngjìbù]	register book	双人间 [shuāngrénjiān]	double room
预订 [yùdìng]	book in advance	标准间 [biāozhǔnjiān]	standard room
证件 [zhèngjiàn]	I.D. documents	空房间 [kōng fángjiān]	vacant room
身份证 [shēnfènzhèng]	identity card	套间 [tàojiān]	suite
护照 [hùzhào]	passport	会议室 [huìyìshì]	meeting room
押金 [yājīn]	deposit	商务中心 [shāngwù zhōngxīn]	business center
房卡 [fángkǎ]	room card	娱乐中心 [yúlè zhōngxīn]	entertainment center
入住 [rùzhù]	check in	餐厅 [cāntīng]	dining room
退房 [tuì fáng]	check out	电梯 [diàntī]	elevator; lift
结账 [jiézhàng]	pay the bill	走廊 [zǒuláng]	corridor

When are you going to check in?
您打算什么时候入住？ Nín dǎsuàn shénme shíhou rùzhù?

I'm going to check in on May 7.
我打算五月七号入住。 Wǒ dǎsuàn Wǔyuè qī hào rùzhù.

	①	②	③	④
	Subjective 主体	Mentality 心态	Time 时间	Action 行动
	You(with respect) 您 [nín]	be going to 打算 [dǎsuàn]	when 什么时候 [shénme shíhou] on May 7 五月七号 [Wǔyuè qī hào]	check in 入住 [rùzhù]
	You 你 [nǐ]		on August 7 八月七号 [Bāyuè qī hào]	
	I 我 [wǒ]		on November 1 十一月一号 [Shíyīyuè yī hào]	
	We 我们 [wǒmen]	want to 想 [xiǎng]	on Friday of next week 下星期五 [xià Xīngqīwǔ]	check out 退房 [tuì fáng]
Sentence Making 造句 [zàojù]	When do you want to check out? I want to check out on Friday next week.		你想什么时候退房？ 我想下星期五退房。	

Notes 注解

The radical "亻" is the changed form of "人 [rén] (human being)". It is called "单人旁 [dānrénpáng]". Sinograms with the radical "亻" have meanings related to "human being" and "activities of human beings". As far as the siongram "住 [zhù] (live)" is concerned, its radical is "亻" because the related subjective is human being. As for the sinogram "宿 [sù] (dormitory)", its radical is "宀 (the shape is like a roof, it is the top part of 家 [jiā] (house)," because the living place of human beings is a house. The radical "宀" is called "家字头 [jiāzìtóu]". Sinograms with the radical "宀" express the meaning related to "house, room", i.e., "housing for living in".

字基 (部首)"亻"是"人"的变体，叫做"单人旁"。凡是"亻 (单人旁)"的字都有"人和人的活动"的意思。"住"着眼于"住的主体是人"，所以"住"字的字基 (部首) 是"亻 (单人旁)"。而"宿"着眼于"宿的地点是家"，所以"宿"字的字基 (部首) 是"宀" (形状像"屋顶"，是"家"字的上头)，叫做"家字头"。凡是"宀 (家字头)"的字都有"家、室、宅"的意思，就是"可以住宿的房屋"的意思。

Vocabulary 词语

人 [rén]	person; human being	家 [jiā]	home; house; family
从 [cóng]	follow	室 [shì]	room
信 [xìn]	believe	宅 [zhái]	residence
住 [zhù]	live	宿 [sù]	dormitory; hostel; sleep
伙 [huǒ]	partner	宝 [bǎo]	treasure
伴 [bàn]	companion	灾 [zāi]	disaster

How long did he sleep last Friday?

他上星期五睡了多长时间？ Tā shàng Xīngqīwǔ shuìle duō cháng shíjiān?

054

He slept for 4 hours last Friday.

他上星期五睡了四个小时。 Tā shàng Xīngqīwǔ shuìle sì gè xiǎoshí.

① Subjective 主体	② Time 时间	③ Verbal 述谓		④ Duration 时量
		Action 行动	Postpositive 后助词	
you 你 [nǐ]	last Friday 上星期五 [shàng Xīngqīwǔ]	sleep 睡 [shuì]		how long 多长时间 [duō cháng shíjiān]
he 他 [tā]				for four hours 四个小时 [sì gè xiǎoshí]
she 她 [tā]			{　} 了 [le]	for a long time 很久 [hěnjiǔ]
Li Fen 李芬 [Lǐ Fēn]	yesterday 昨天 [zuótiān]	rest 休息 [xiūxi]		for more than half an hour 半个多钟头 [bàn gè duō zhōngtóu]
Sentence Making 造句 [zàojù]	How long did Li Fen rest yesterday? She rested for more than half an hour yesterday.			**李芬昨天休息了多长时间？** 她昨天休息了半个多钟头。

Notes 注解

"Time" indicates the point of time when the action happens. "Duration" indicates the period of time the action lasts. The word order of a Chinese sentence is "subjective +time + action + duration".

"时间"指行动发生的"时点"。"时量"指行动持续的"时段"。汉语的顺序是"主体+时间+行动+时量"。

Vocabulary 词语

睡 [shuì]	sleep	时间 [shíjiān]	time
睡觉 [shuìjiào]	sleep	时点 [shí diǎn]	point of time
睡着了 [shuìzháo le]	fell asleep	时量 [shíliàng]	duration
酣睡 [hān shuì]	sleep soundly	时段 [shíduàn]	period of time
瞌睡 [kēshuì]	sleepy; drowsy	发生 [fāshēng]	happen
睡眼 [shuì yǎn]	drowsy eyes	持续 [chíxù]	lasting; sustain; continue
睡意 [shuìyì]	sleepiness	结束 [jiéshù]	end
小睡 [xiǎoshuì]	nap	卧 [wò]	lie down
睡眠 [shuìmián]	sleeping	仰卧 [yǎngwò]	lie on one's back
不眠 [bù mián]	sleepless	侧卧 [cèwò]	lie on one's side
失眠 [shīmián]	insomnia	俯卧 [fǔwò]	lie on one's stomach

What is there in the room?
房间里有什么？ Fángjiān li yǒu shénme?

There is an air conditioner in the room.
房间里有空调。Fángjiān li yǒu kōngtiáo.

	① Location 地点	② Existing 存在	③ Subjective 主体
	room 房间 [fángjiān]		what 什么 [shénme]
			air conditioner 空调 [kōngtián]
	in 里 [li]	there be (is/are) 有 [yǒu]	TV set 电视 [diànshì]
			refrigerator 冰箱 [bīngxiāng]
	bedroom 卧室 [wòshì]		bed 床 [chuáng]
Sentence Making 造句 [zàojù]	What is there in the bedroom? There is a bed in the bedroom.	卧室里有什么? 卧室里有床。	

Vocabulary 词语

房间设施 [fángjiān shèshī]	room facilities	电视 [diànshì]	TV set
空调 [kōngtiáo]	air conditioner	遥控器 [yáokòngqì]	remote control
地毯 [dìtǎn]	carpet	冰箱 [bīngxiāng]	refrigerator
家具 [jiāju]	furniture	沙发 [shāfā]	sofa
床 [chuáng]	bed	茶几 [chájī]	tea table
单人床 [dānrénchuáng]	single bed	烟灰缸 [yānhuīgāng]	ashtray
双人床 [shuāngrénchuáng]	double bed	垃圾桶 [lājītǒng]	garbage bin
被子 [bèizi]	quilt	马桶 [mǎtǒng]	toilet (appliance)
褥子 [rùzi]	mattress	浴缸 [yùgāng]	bathtub
毛毯 [máotǎn]	blanket	浴帽 [yùmào]	bathing cap
床单 [chuángdān]	bed sheet	浴巾 [yùjīn]	bath towel
枕头 [zhěntou]	pillow	牙刷 [yáshuā]	toothbrush
拖鞋 [tuōxié]	slippers	牙膏 [yágāo]	toothpaste
衣柜 [yīguì]	wardrobe; closet	梳妆台 [shūzhuāngtái]	dresser
台灯 [táidēng]	reading lamp	梳子 [shūzi]	comb

Which direction do those windows face?
那些窗子朝哪个方向？ Nàxiē chuāngzi cháo nǎge fāngxiàng?

Those windows face toward the south.
那些窗子朝南。 Nàxiē chuāngzi cháo nán.

① Subjective 主体		② Linking 联系	③ Relative 系体
Determiner 限定	Substance 实体		
those 那些 [nàxiē]	window 窗子 [chuāngzi]		which direction 哪个方向 [nǎge fāngxiàng]
			south 南 [nán]
of that room 那个房间的 [nàge fángjiān de]	door 门 [mén]	face toward 朝 [cháo]	northwest 西北 [xīběi]
of that courtyard 那个院子的 [nàge yuànzi de]	main gate 大门 [dàmén]		southeast 东南 [dōngnán]
Sentence Making 造句 [zàojù]	Which direction does the main gate of that courtyard face? The main gate of that courtyard faces the southeast.		那个院子的大门朝哪个方向？ 那个院子的大门朝东南。

Notes 注解

In Chinese, "east" and "west" are put before "south" and "north" as far as directions are concerned. In English it is the opposite. For example in Chinese people say "东北 [dōngběi] and 西南 [xīnán]," while in English they are expressed as northeast and southwest.

汉语谈到"方向"，先说"东"、"西"，后说"南"、"北"。如汉语说"东北、西南"，而英语说"northeast, southwest"。

Vocabulary 词语

门 [mén]	gate	方向 [fāngxiàng]	direction
大门 [dàmén]	main gate	朝 [cháo]	face; toward
边门 [biānmén]	side gate	东 [dōng]	east
球门 [qiúmén]	goal (for football)	西 [xī]	west
门环 [ménhuán]	door ring	南 [nán]	south
门坎 [ménkǎn]	threshold	北 [běi]	north
窗子 [chuāngzi]	window	东南 [dōngnán]	southeast
橱窗 [chúchuāng]	show window	东北 [dōngběi]	northeast
天窗 [tiānchuāng]	skylight	西南 [xīnán]	southwest
窗扇 [chuāngshàn]	window sash	西北 [xīběi]	northwest

By whom was your room card lost?
你们的房卡被谁弄丢了？ Nǐmen de fángkǎ bèi shuí nòngdiū le?

Our room card was lost by my son.
我们的房卡被我儿子弄丢了。 Wǒmen de fángkǎ bèi wǒ érzi nòngdiū le.

① Objective 客体		② Subjective 主体		③ Verbal 述谓	
Determiner 限定	Substance 实体	Prepositive 前辅词	Substance 实体	Action 行动	Postpositive 后助词
your(pl.) 你们的 [nǐmen de]	room card 房卡 [fángkǎ]		who/whom 谁 [shuí]	lose 弄丢 [nòngdiū]	
your 你的 [nǐ de]			my son 我儿子 [wǒ érzi]		
our 我们的 [wǒmen de]	glasses 眼镜 [yǎnjìng]	by 被 [bèi]	him 他 [tā]	break 弄破 [nòngpò]	{ } 了 [le]
my 我的 [wǒ de]	cell phone 手机 [shǒujī]		Li Ming 李明 [Lǐ Míng]	take away 拿走 [názǒu]	
Sentence Making 造句 [zàojù]	By whom was my cell phone taken away? Your cell phone was taken away by Li Ming.			我的手机被谁拿走了？ 你的手机被李明拿走了。	

Notes 注解

The main frame of English sentences is "subject+ predicate." It requires the agreement of subject and predicate verb. Chinese doesn't require the agreement of subjective and predicate verb.

The main frame of Chinese sentences is "topic + comment." "Topic" comprises the first topic and the second topic. They are all put before the predicate verb. A Chinese sentence that uses the word "被 [bèi] (by)" takes the preconceived objective as the first topic, and takes the subjective after "被 [bèi] (by)" as the second topic.

英语句子以"主语＋谓语"为主要框架，要求"主语谓语的一致关系"。汉语没有"主语谓语的一致关系"，句子以"话题 (Topic) ＋述题 (Comment)"为主要框架。"话题"分为"第一话题"和"第二话题"，都位于谓语动词之前。汉语"被"字句是以预想的"客体"作为"第一话题"，以"被"字引出的"主体"作为"第二话题"的句式。

Vocabulary 词语

卡 [kǎ]	card	证 [zhèng]	certificate; card
信用卡 [xìnyòngkǎ]	credit card	学生证 [xuéshengzhèng]	student identity card
交通卡 [jiāotōngkǎ]	transportation card	居留证 [jūliúzhèng]	residence card
购物卡 [gòuwùkǎ]	shopping card	借书证 [jièshūzhèng]	library card
会员卡 [huìyuánkǎ]	membership card	驾驶证 [jiàshǐzhèng]	driving license
胸卡 [xiōngkǎ]	chest card	营业证 [yíngyèzhèng]	business license
贺卡 [hèkǎ]	greeting card	签证 [qiānzhèng]	visa

How do you want your hair to be cut?
你想把头发剪成什么样? Nǐ xiǎng bǎ tóufa jiǎn chéng shénme yàng?

I'd like to have my hair cut shorter.
我想把头发剪短点儿。 Wǒ xiǎng bǎ tóufa jiǎnduǎn diǎnr.

①	②	③	④	
Subjective 主体	Verbal 1 述谓 1	Objective 客体	Verbal 2 述谓 2	
	Mentality 心态		Action 行动	State 状态
you 你 [nǐ]	would like to 想 [xiǎng]	hair 【把头发】 [bǎ tóufa]	cut 剪 [jiǎn]	how (what is it like) 什么样 [shénme yàng]
				shorter 短点儿 [duǎn diǎnr]
you(polite) 您 [nín]			{成 [chéng]}	longer 长点儿 [cháng diǎnr]
			dye 染 [rǎn]	what color 什么颜色 [shénme yánsè]
I 我 [wǒ]	want to 要 [yào]			yellow 黄色 [huángsè]
Sentence Making 造句 [zàojù]	What color would you like to dye your hair? I want to dye my hair yellow.		你想把头发染成什么颜色? 我要把头发染成黄色。	

Notes 注解

The Chinese "把 [bǎ]" sentence is a kind of sentence frame which takes the preconceived objective as the second topic. The preconceived objective is in the state of being handled and it is put before the verb. The result of the handling is shown as the new state of the objective after the verb.

汉语的"把"字句是表示"预想"的待处理的"客体"作为"第二话题"而位于谓语动词之前的句式。处理的"结果"表现为动词之后的"新状态"。

Vocabulary 词语

头发 [tóufa]	hair	发型 [fàxíng]	hairstyle
须发 [xūfà]	beard and hair	发卡 [fàqiǎ]	hairpin
鬓发 [bìnfà]	hair over the temples	发网 [fàwǎng]	hairnet
理发 [lǐfà]	haircut	发胶 [fàjiāo]	hairspray
烫发 [tàngfà]	perm	洗头 [xǐtóu]	wash one's hair
染发 [rǎnfà]	dye hair	吹风 [chuīfēng]	dry one's hair
卷发 [juǎnfà]	curly hair	焗油 [júyóu]	treat one's hair with cream
假发 [jiǎfà]	wig	美容 [měiróng]	beauty treatment
护发素 [hùfàsù]	hair conditioner	面膜 [miànmó]	facial mask

What trees are there in this residential quarter?
这个住宅区里有什么树？ Zhège zhùzháiqū li yǒu shénme shù?

There are many pines in this residential quarter.
这个住宅区里有很多松树。 Zhège zhùzháiqū li yǒu hěn duō sōngshù.

① Location 地点			② Existing 存在	③ Subjective 主体	
Determiner 限定	Place 处所	Postpositive 后助词		Amount 数量	Substance 实体
this 这个 [zhège]	residential quarter 住宅区 [zhùzháiqū]			what tree 什么树 [shénme shù]	
		in {里 [li]}	there be 有 [yǒu]	some 一些 [yìxiē]	pine 松树 [sōngshù]
					willow 柳树 [liǔshù]
that 那个 [nàge]	park 公园 [gōngyuán]			many 很多 [hěn duō]	cherry tree 樱桃树 [yīngtaoshù]
Sentence Making 造句 [zàojù]	What trees are there in this residential quarter? There are some cherry trees in this residential quarter.			这个住宅区里有什么树？ 这个住宅区里有一些樱桃树。	

Notes 注解

The radical "木" is the changed form of "木 [mù] (tree)". It is called "木字旁 [mùzìpáng]". Sinograms with the radical "木" have meanings related to "tree, wood or wooden product".

字基(部首) "木" 是 "木" 的变体，叫做 "木字旁"。凡有字基(部首) "木" 的字都跟 "树、木及木制品" 的意思有关。

Vocabulary 词语

木 [mù]	tree; timber; wood	杆 [gān]	shaft; pole
林 [lín]	woods; forest	杠 [gàng]	thick rod
森林 [sēnlín]	forest	柱 [zhù]	pillar
树 [shù]	tree	板 [bǎn]	board
枝 [zhī]	branch	柜 [guì]	closet; cabinet
根 [gēn]	root	栏 [lán]	bar
杨树 [yángshù]	poplar	桥 [qiáo]	bridge
柳树 [liǔshù]	willow	梯 [tī]	stair
松树 [sōngshù]	pine	棋 [qí]	chess
槐树 [huáishù]	pagoda tree	棚 [péng]	awning
榆树 [yúshù]	elm	楼 [lóu]	building

What flowers are there in this flower bed?
这个花坛里有什么花？ Zhège huātán li yǒu shénme huā?

There are many red roses in this flower bed.
这个花坛里有很多红玫瑰。 Zhège huātán li yǒu hěn duō hóng méigui.

①			②	③		
Location 地点			Existing 存在	Subjective 主体		
Determiner 限定	Place 处所	Postpositive 后助词		Amount 数量	Attribute 属性	Substance 实物
this 这个 [zhège]	flower bed 花坛 [huātán]			what flower 什么花 [shénme huā]		
				many 很多 [hěn duō]	red 红 [hóng]	rose 玫瑰 [méigui]
		in {里 [li]}	there be 有 [yǒu]		white 白 [bái]	
that 那个 [nàge]	flower garden 花园 [huāyuán]			some 一些 [yìxiē]	yellow 黄 [huáng]	chrysanthemum 菊花 [júhuā]
Sentence Making 造句 [zàojù]	What flowers are there in that park? There are some yellow chrysanthemums in that park.			那个公园里有什么花？ 那个公园里有一些黄菊花。		

Notes 注解

The radical " 艹 " is the top part of " 草 [cǎo] (grass)". It is called " 草字头 [cǎozìtóu]". Sinograms with the radical " 艹 " have meanings related to "grass or flower".

字基(部首) " 艹 " 是 "草" 字的上头，叫做 "草字头"。凡是有 " 艹 (草字头)" 的字都跟 "草、花" 的意思有关。

Vocabulary 词语

草 [cǎo]	grass	葫芦 [húlu]	gourd
芽 [yá]	sprout	荸荠 [bíqi]	water chestnut
花 [huā]	flower	芦苇 [lúwěi]	reed
苞 [bāo]	bud	莲藕 [lián'ǒu]	lotus root
蕊 [ruǐ]	stamen; pistil	蘑菇 [mógu]	mushroom
荷 [hé]	lotus	茉莉 [mòli]	jasmine
苗 [miáo]	seedling	葡萄 [pútɑo]	grape
茎 [jìng]	stem	芭蕉 [bājiāo]	Japanese banana
苔 [tái]	lichen; moss	菠萝 [bōluó]	pineapple
药 [yào]	medicine; herb	芬芳 [fēnfāng]	fragrant; fragrance

VII

Transportation
交通 [jiāotōng]

061. Where are you going? 您到哪里去？　　　I am going to Guangzhou. 我到广州去。

062. Where did you come from? 您从哪里来？　　　I came from Chongqing. 我从重庆来。

063. What is the weather like tomorrow? 明天天气怎么样？

It will be sunny tomorrow, 18 degrees to 29 degrees. 明天晴天，十八度到二十九度。

064. Have you ever been to Beijing before？您以前曾经到过北京吗？

I have never been to Beijing before. 我以前没有到过北京。

065. Where would you like to go? 你想去哪里？

I'd like to go to Beijing Hotel. 我想去北京饭店。

066. How should we go? 我们应该怎么去？　　　You can go by subway. 你们可以坐地铁去。

067. Which bus should I take to go to the Fragrant Hills? 我去香山该坐几路公交车？

You should take bus No. 968 to go to the Fragrant Hills. 您去香山该坐 968 路公交车。

068. Where is the subway station? 地铁站在哪里？

The subway station is in front. 地铁站在前边。

069. What ticket would you like to book? 您想订什么票？

I'd like to book an air ticket to Shanghai for tomorrow. 我想订一张明天去上海的机票。

070. What would you like to send? 你想寄什么？　　　I'd like to send a registered letter. 我想寄挂号信。

Where are you going?
您到哪里去？ Nín dào nǎli qù?

I am going to Guangzhou.
我到广州去。 Wǒ dào Guǎngzhōu qù.

①	②		③
	Location 地点		
Subjective 主体	Prepositive 前辅词	Place 处所	Action 行动
you(polite) 您 [nín]		where 哪里 [nǎli]	
you 你 [nǐ]		Guangzhou 广州 [Guǎngzhōu]	go 去 [qù]
I 我 [wǒ]	to 到 [dào]	Wuhan 武汉 [Wǔhàn]	
her friend 她的朋友 [tā de péngyou]		Jiangsu 江苏 [Jiāngsū]	
Sentence Making 造句 [zàojù]	Where are you going? I am going to Jiangsu.		你到哪里去? 我到江苏去。

Notes 注解

There are four municipalities in China: Beijing (北京 [Běijīng]), Tianjin (天津 [Tiānjīn]), Shanghai (上海 [Shànghǎi]) and Chongqing (重庆 [Chóngqìng]).

There are two special administrative regions: Hong Kong (香港 [Xiānggǎng]) and Macao (澳门 [Àomén]).

In the following table are the Chinese provinces, the autonomous regions, and their capital cities.

中国有4个直辖市：北京、天津、上海、重庆。中国有两个特别行政区：香港、澳门。

中国的各省、自治区及其首府见下表。

省和自治区 [shěng hé zìzhìqū]	Provinces and Autonomous Regions	首府 [shǒufǔ]	Capital Cities
河北 [Héběi]	Hebei	石家庄 [Shíjiāzhuāng]	Shijiazhuang
山西 [Shānxī]	Shanxi	太原 [Tàiyuán]	Taiyuan
内蒙古 [Nèiměnggǔ]	Inner Mongolia	呼和浩特 [Hūhéhàotè]	Hohhot
辽宁 [Liáoníng]	Liaoning	沈阳 [Shěnyáng]	Shenyang
吉林 [Jílín]	Jilin	长春 [Chángchūn]	Changchun
黑龙江 [Hēilóngjiāng]	Heilongjiang	哈尔滨 [Hā'ěrbīn]	Harbin
山东 [Shāndōng]	Shandong	济南 [Jǐnán]	Jinan
安徽 [Ānhuī]	Anhui	合肥 [Héféi]	Hefei
江苏 [Jiāngsū]	Jiangsu	南京 [Nánjīng]	Nanjing
浙江 [Zhèjiāng]	Zhejiang	杭州 [Hángzhōu]	Hangzhou
江西 [Jiāngxī]	Jiangxi	南昌 [Nánchāng]	Nanchang
福建 [Fújiàn]	Fujian	福州 [Fúzhōu]	Fuzhou
台湾 [Táiwān]	Taiwan	台北 [Táiběi]	Taipei

(To be continued　待续)

Where did you come from?

您从哪里来? Nín cóng nǎli lái?

I came from Chongqing.

我从重庆来。Wǒ cóng Chóngqìng lái.

① Subjective 主体	② Location 地点		③ Action 行动
	Prepositive 前辅词	Place 处所	
you(polite) 您 [nín]		where 哪里 [nǎli]	
you 你 [nǐ]	from 从 [cóng]	Chongqing 重庆 [Chóngqìng]	come 来 [lái]
I 我 [wǒ]		Guangzhou 广州 [Guǎngzhōu]	
that boy 那个男孩儿 [nàge nánháir]		Jiangsu 江苏 [Jiāngsū]	
Sentence Making 造句 [zàojù]	Where did that boy come from? He came from Jiangsu.	那个男孩儿从哪里来? 他从江苏来。	

(Continued 续)

省和自治区 [shěng hé zìzhìqū]	Provinces and Autonomous Regions	首府 [shǒufǔ]	Capital Cities
河南 [Hénán]	Henan	郑州 [Zhèngzhōu]	Zhengzhou
湖北 [Húběi]	Hubei	武汉 [Wǔhàn]	Wuhan
湖南 [Húnán]	Hunan	长沙 [Chángshā]	Changsha
广东 [Guǎngdōng]	Guangdong	广州 [Guǎngzhōu]	Guangzhou
广西 [Guǎngxī]	Guangxi	南宁 [Nánníng]	Naning
海南 [Hǎinán]	Hainan	海口 [Hǎikǒu]	Haikou
四川 [Sìchuān]	Sichuan	成都 [Chéngdū]	Chengdu
贵州 [Guìzhōu]	Guizhou	贵阳 [Guìyáng]	Guiyang
云南 [Yúnnán]	Yunnan	昆明 [Kūnmíng]	Kunming
西藏 [Xīzàng]	Tibet	拉萨 [Lāsà]	Lhasa
陕西 [Shǎnxī]	Shaanxi	西安 [Xī' ān]	Xi'an
甘肃 [Gānsù]	Gansu	兰州 [Lánzhōu]	Lanzhou
青海 [Qīnghǎi]	Qinghai	西宁 [Xīníng]	Xi'ning
宁夏 [Níngxià]	Ningxia	银川 [Yínchuān]	Yinchuan
新疆 [Xīnjiāng]	Xinjiang	乌鲁木齐 [Wūlǔmùqí]	Urumchi

What is the weather like tomorrow?
明天天气怎么样？ Míngtiān tiānqì zěnmeyàng?

It will be sunny tomorrow, 18 degrees to 29 degrees.
明天晴天，十八度到二十九度。 Míngtiān qíngtiān, shíbā dù dào èrshíjiǔ dù.

① Subjective 主体		② Linking 联系	③ Relative 系体	
Time 时间	Phenomenon 现象			
tomorrow 明天 [míngtiān]	weather { 天气 [tiānqì] }		what is it like 怎么样 ?[zěnmeyàng]	
		be { }	sunny 晴天 [qíngtiān]	18 degrees to 29 degrees 十八度到二十九度 [shíbā dù dào èrshíjiǔ dù]
			rain 下雨 [xiàyǔ]	9 degrees to 16 degrees 九度到十六度 [jiǔ dù dào shíliù dù]
			snow 下雪 [xiàxuě]	10 degrees below zero to 0 degree 零下十度到零度 ?[língxià shí dù dào líng dù]
today 今天 [jīntiān]	it { }		cloudy 多云 [duōyún]	
Sentence Making 造句 [zàojù]	What is the weather like today? It is snowing, 10 degrees below zero to 0 degree.		今天天气怎么样？ 今天下雪，零下十度到零度。	

Notes　注解

Sinograms with the radical "⻗ (雨字头) [yǔzìtóu]" all have the meaning of "rain and precipitation" .

字基(部首)是 "⻗ (雨字头)" 的字都有 "雨和降水" 的意思。

Vocabulary　词语

天气 [tiānqì]	weather	雨 [yǔ]	rain
温度 [wēndù]	temperature	雪 [xuě]	snow
湿度 [shīdù]	humidity	霜 [shuāng]	frost
晴 [qíng]	clear; fine; sunny	雹 [báo]	hail
阴 [yīn]	overcast	雾 [wù]	fog
云 [yún]	cloud	霾 [mái]	haze
多云 [duōyún]	cloudy	露 [lù]	dew
风 [fēng]	wind	雷 [léi]	thunder
台风 [táifēng]	typhoon	霞 [xiá]	rosy cloud
风暴 [fēngbào]	storm	霉 [méi]	mildew
沙尘暴 [shāchénbào]	sandstorm	霹雳 [pīlì]	thunderbolt

Have you ever been to Beijing before?
您以前曾经到过北京吗? Nín yǐqián céngjīng dàoguo Běijīng ma?

I have never been to Beijing before.
我以前没有到过北京。Wǒ yǐqián méiyǒu dàoguo Běijīng.

① Subjective 主体	② Time 时间	③ Verbal 述谓			④ Goal 终点	⑤ Postpositive 后助词
		Prepositive 前辅词	Action 行动	Postpositive 后助词		
you(polite) 您 [nín]		ever 曾经 [céngjīng]	be 到 [dào]		Beijing 北京 [Běijīng]	
you 你 [nǐ]	before 以前 [yǐqián]			{ } 过 [guo]	China 中国 [Zhōngguó]	{ } {吗 [ma]}
I 我 [wǒ]		never 没有 [méiyǒu]	visit 游览 [yóulǎn]		the Great Wall 长城 [Chángchéng]	

Sentence Making 造句 [zàojù]	Have you ever visited the Great Wall before? 你以前曾经游览过长城吗? I have never visited the Great Wall before. 我以前没有游览过长城。

Notes 注解

1. The postpositive "过 [guo]" added after verbs indicates experiences that have happened before. The negative form of this kind of sentence has to put "没 [méi]" before the verb, and "不 [bù]" shouldn't be used instead of "没 [méi]."

2. The radical "扌(土字旁 [tǔzìpáng])" and "土 (土字底 [tǔzìdǐ])" have the meaning of "soil and building with soil." The earliest wall and city wall were not built of bricks but soil. Therefore, "墙 [qiáng] (wall), and 城 [chéng] (city)" both have the radical "扌(土字旁)" on the left. "壁 [bì] (wall), and 堡 [bǎo] (fortress)" both have the radical "土 (土字底)" on the bottom.

1. 后助词"过"加在动词之后表示"实际发生过的经历"。对"经历"的否定只能用"没",不能用"不"。

2. 字基(部首)"扌(土字旁)"和"土 (土字底)"的字都有"土地和泥土建筑物"的意思。最早的墙和城都不是用"砖"筑成的,而是用"土"筑成的。所以,"墙、城"都是"扌(土字旁)","壁、堡"都是"土 (土字底)"。

Vocabulary 词语

天安门广场 [Tiān'ānmén Guǎngchǎng]	Tian'anmen Square	土 [tǔ]	soil; ground; land
故宫博物院 [Gùgōng Bówùyuàn]	Palace Museum	场 [chǎng]	site; spot
颐和园 [Yíhéyuán]	Summer Palace	坡 [pō]	slope
天坛 [Tiāntán]	the Temple of Heaven	墙 [qiáng]	wall
长城 [Chángchéng]	the Great Wall	城 [chéng]	city; wall; urban
八达岭 [Bādálǐng]	the Great Wall at Badaling	塔 [tǎ]	tower
明十三陵 [Míng Shísānlíng]	Ming Tombs	壁 [bì]	wall
北京植物园 [Běijīng Zhíwùyuán]	Beijing Botanical Garden	堡 [bǎo]	fortress

Where would you like to go?
你想去哪里？ Nǐ xiǎng qù nǎli?

I'd like to go to Beijing Hotel.
我想去北京饭店。 Wǒ xiǎng qù Běijīng Fàndiàn.

① Subjective 主体	② Verbal 述谓		③ Goal 终点
	Mentality 心态	Action 行动	
you 你 [nǐ]	would like to 想 [xiǎng]		where 哪里 [nǎli]
I 我 [wǒ]		go 去 [qù]	to { }	Beijing Hotel 北京饭店 [Běijīng Fàndiàn] Summer Palace 颐和园 [Yíhéyuán] Tian'anmen Square 天安门广场 [Tiān'ānmén Guǎngchǎng]
you(polite) 您 [nín]	want to 要 [yào]		
Sentence Making 造句 [zàojù]	Where do you want to go? I want to go to Tian'anmen Square.		你要去哪里？ 我要去天安门广场。

Notes 注解

The meaning of the radical "广" is not the meaning of "广阔 [guǎngkuò] (wide)" but "roof; the top of a building". The radical "广" is called "库字头 [kùzìtóu](top part of 库)". The top part of the sinogram "库" is "广 [guǎng] (roof)" and the bottom part is "车 [chē] (wheeled vehicle)." The place with a roof to park wheeled vehicles is called "库 [kù] (storehouse)". Later the meaning was expanded to indicate "a house to keep things."

字基(部首) "广" 的意义不是 "广阔" ，而是 "房顶" ，叫做 "库字头" 。"库" 字上部为 "广(房顶)" ，下部为 "车" ，表示有 "房顶" 的存放 "车" 的地方叫做 "库" 。后来字义扩大为 "存放物品的房屋" 叫做 "库" 。

Vocabulary 词语

库 [kù]	storehouse; depository	车库 [chēkù]	garage
店 [diàn]	shop	书店 [shūdiàn]	bookstore
府 [fǔ]	official residence	政府 [zhèngfǔ]	government
庄 [zhuāng]	village	山庄 [shānzhuāng]	mountain village
庭 [tíng]	hall	法庭 [fǎtíng]	court
座 [zuò]	seat	茶座 [cházuò]	tea house
席 [xí]	mat; seat; feast; banquet	首席 [shǒuxí]	seat of honor; chief
廊 [láng]	corridor	长廊 [chángláng]	gallery; long corridor

How should we go?
我们应该怎么去？ Wǒmen yīnggāi zěnme qù?

You can go by subway.
你们可以坐地铁去。 Nǐmen kěyǐ zuò dìtiě qù.

① Subjective 主体	② Verbal 述谓 / Prepositive 前辅词	③ Manner 方式		④ Verbal 述谓 / Action 行动
we 我们 [wǒmen]	should 应该 [yīnggāi]	how 怎么 [zěnme]		
you 你们 [nǐmen]	may 可以 [kěyǐ]	by 坐 [zuò]	subway 地铁 [dìtiě]	go 去 [qù]
			taxi 出租车 [chūzūchē]	
they 他们 [tāmen]	shall/will 要 [yào]		bus 公交车 [gōngjiāochē]	
Sentence Making 造句 [zàojù]	How should we go? You can go by bus.	我们应该怎么去？ 你们可以坐公交车去。		

Notes 注解

A family of multisyllabic words can be formed by using the classifying sinogram "车 [chē] (wheeled vehicle)" to indicate all kinds of wheeled vehicles.

类别字"车"可以构成一族"多字词"来表示各种各样的"××车"。

Vocabulary 词语

车 [chē]	wheeled vehicle	公交车 [gōngjiāochē]	bus
轿车 [jiàochē]	car	出租车 [chūzūchē]	taxi
火车 [huǒchē]	train	救护车 [jiùhùchē]	ambulance
电车 [diànchē]	trolley bus	自行车 [zìxíngchē]	bicycle
卡车 [kǎchē]	truck	三轮车 [sānlúnchē]	tricycle
叉车 [chāchē]	forklift	独轮车 [dúlúnchē]	wheelbarrow
吊车 [diàochē]	crane	牵引车 [qiānyǐnchē]	tractor
机车 [jīchē]	locomotive	洒水车 [sǎshuǐchē]	sprinkler
拖车 [tuōchē]	trailer	消防车 [xiāofángchē]	fire engine
风车 [fēngchē]	windmill	人力车 [rénlìchē]	rickshaw
水车 [shuǐchē]	waterwheel; water mill	加油车 [jiāyóuchē]	refueller

Which bus should I take to go to the Fragrant Hills?
我去香山该坐几路公交车？ Wǒ qù Xiāngshān gāi zuò jǐ lù gōngjiāochē?

You should take Bus No.698 to go to the Fragrant Hills.
您去香山该坐698路公交车。 Nín qù Xiāngshān yūi zuò liùjiǔbā lù gōngjiāochē.

① Subjective 主体	② Purpose 目的		③ Verbal 述谓		④ Objective 客体
	Action 行动	Goal 终点	Prepositive 前辅词	Action 行动	
I 我 [wǒ]		the Fragrant Hills 香山 [Xiāngshān]			which bus 几路公交车 [jǐ lù gōngjiāochē]
	go 去 [qù]	the Yuquan Hills 玉泉山 [Yùquánshān]	should 该 [gāi]	take 坐 [zuò]	Bus No.968 698 路公交车 [liùjiǔbā lù gōngjiāochē]
you(polite) 您 [nín]		the Babao Hills 八宝山 [Bābǎoshān]			Bus No.337 337 路公交车 [sānsānqī lù gōngjiāochē]
Sentence Making 造句 [zàojù]	Which bus I should take to go to the Babao Hills? You should take Bus No.337 to go to the Babao Hills.			我去八宝山应该坐几路公交车？ 您去八宝山应该坐 337 路公交车。	

Notes 注解

1. The radical "屮" is called "山字旁 [shānzìpáng]". It is the changed form of "山 [shān] (mountain)". Sinograms with the radical "屮" all have meanings related to "山 (mountain)".

2. The radical "阝" is called "陆字旁 [lùzìpáng]". It is the left part of "陆 [lù] (land)". Sinograms with the radical "阝" all have meanings related to "小山 [xiǎoshān](small hill)". In people's eyes, a hill is a piece of land protruding from the sea. The slope the sun can illuminate is called "阳 [yáng] ", and the slope that the sun cannot illuminate is called "阴 [yīn]".

1. 字基(部首) "屮" ("山"的变体)，叫做"山字旁"。凡是"屮 (山字旁)"的字义都跟"山 (mountain)"有关。

2. 字基(部首) "阝" ("陆"的左偏旁)，叫做"陆字旁"。凡是"阝(陆字旁)"的字都跟"小山 (hill)"有关。"小山"在人们眼中是海里凸起的一个"陆"地。日光照到的山坡叫做"阳"，日光照不到的山坡叫做"阴"。

Vocabulary 词语

岭 [lǐng]	mountain; mountain range	陆 [lù]	land
峰 [fēng]	peak	阳 [yáng]	sun; the side illuminated by the sun
峻 [jùn]	high	阴 [yīn]	cloudy; the side not illuminated by the sun
峭 [qiào]	high and steep	障 [zhàng]	obstacle
峡 [xiá]	gorge	险 [xiǎn]	dangerous
岗 [gāng]	hillock	陡 [dǒu]	steep
岸 [àn]	bank	隔 [gé]	separate
岩 [yán]	rock; crag	防 [fáng]	protect against

Where is the subway station?
地铁站在哪里？ Dìtiězhàn zài nǎli?

The subway station is in front.
地铁站在前边。 Dìtiězhàn zài qiánbian.

① Subjective 主体	② Existing 存在	③ Location 地点
subway station 地铁站 [dìtiězhàn]		where 哪里 [nǎli]
bus stop 公交车站 [gōngjiāo chēzhàn]		in front 前边 [qiánbian]
gas station 加油站 [jiāyóuzhàn]	be 在 [zài]	on the left 左边 [zuǒbian]
post office 邮局 [yóujú]		over there 那边 [nàbian]
Bank of China 中国银行 [Zhōngguó Yínháng]		at the crossroad 十字路口 [shízìlùkǒu]
Sentence Making 造句 [zàojù]	Where is the Bank of China? The Bank of China is at the crossroad.	中国银行在哪里？ 中国银行在十字路口。

Notes 注解

The radical "辶" is called "运字旁 [yùnzìpáng]". Sinograms with the radical "辶" all have meanings related to "运行 [yùnxíng] (transport)" or "道路 [dàolù] (road)".

字基(部首)是 "辶 (运字旁)" 的字都跟 "运行" 或 "道路" 的意思有关。

Vocabulary 词语

火车站 [huǒchēzhàn]	railway station	运 [yùn]	transport
地铁站 [dìtiězhàn]	subway station	道 [dào]	road; method; line
汽车站 [qìchēzhàn]	bus station	达 [dá]	reach; express
停车场 [tíngchēchǎng]	parking lot	通 [tōng]	be passable; dredge; know
人行道 [rénxíngdào]	side walk	进 [jìn]	enter; move forward
人行横道 [rénxíng héngdào]	crosswalk	退 [tuì]	retreat; return; resign; fade
街 [jiē]	street	返 [fǎn]	return
路 [lù]	road	迎 [yíng]	welcome; towards
过街天桥 [guòjiē tiānqiáo]	overpass	送 [sòng]	deliver; see sb. off
十字路口 [shízì lùkǒu]	crossroads	追 [zhuī]	chase; investigate
立交桥 [lìjiāoqiáo]	flyover	逃 [táo]	escape; flee
人行地下道 [rénxíng dìxiàdào]	underpass	避 [bì]	avoid; evade; shun

What ticket would you like to book?
您想订什么票？ Nín xiǎng dìng shéme piào?

I'd like to book an air ticket to Shanghai for tomorrow.
我想订一张明天去上海的机票。 Wǒ xiǎng dìng yì zhāng míngtiān qù Shànghǎi de jīpiào.

① Subjective 主体	② Action 行动	③ Objective 客体			
		Amount 数量	Time 时间	Goal 终点	Ticket 票
you(polite) 您 [nín]	would like to book 想订 [xiǎng dìng]	what ticket 什么票 [shénme piào]			
		a 一张 [yì zhāng]	for tomorrow 明天 [míngtiān]	Shanghai 上海 [Shànghǎi]	air ticket 机票 [jīpiào]
		four 四张 [sì zhāng]	for next Monday 下周一 [xià zhōuyī]	to 去 [qù] Guangzhou 广州 [Guǎngzhōu]	{ } 的 [de] soft seat ticket 软座票 [ruǎnzuòpiào]
I 我 [wǒ]	want to buy 要买 [yào mǎi]	five 五张 [wǔ zhāng]	for May 8 5月8日 [Wǔyuè bā rì]	Xi'an 西安 [Xī'ān]	hard berth ticket 硬卧票 [yìngwòpiào]
Sentence Making 造句 [zàojù]	What ticket would you like to buy? 您要买什么票？ I want to buy three soft berth tickets to Guangzhou for May 8. 我要买三张5月8日去广州的软卧票。				

Vocabulary 词语

航空 [hángkōng]	airway; aviation	票 [piào]	ticket
民航 [mínháng]	civil airplane	机票 [jīpiào]	air ticket
出航 [chūháng]	launch out	单程票 [dānchéngpiào]	one-way ticket
返航 [fǎnháng]	return to the point of departure	返程票 [fǎnchéngpiào]	return ticket
航线 [hángxiàn]	airline	补票 [bǔpiào]	re-scheduled ticket
航班 [hángbān]	flight	火车票 [huǒchēpiào]	train ticket
航程 [hángchéng]	voyage	站台票 [zhàntáipiào]	platform ticket
航运 [hángyùn]	shipping by water	普快 [pǔkuài]	average express
客舱 [kècāng]	passenger cabin	直快 [zhíkuài]	through express
经济舱 [jīngjìcāng]	economy class	特快 [tèkuài]	super express
头等舱 [tóuděngcāng]	first class	软座 [ruǎnzuò]	soft seat ticket
起飞 [qǐfēi]	take off	硬卧 [yìngwò]	hard sleeper ticket
着陆 [zhuólù]	land	软卧 [ruǎnwò]	soft sleeper ticket
驾驶员 [jiàshǐyuán]	driver	长途车票 [chángtú chēpiào]	coach ticket
乘务员 [chéngwùyuán]	attendant	船票 [chuánpiào]	ship ticket
空姐 [kōngjiě]	air hostess	退票 [tuì piào]	refund ticket

What would you like to send?
您想寄什么? Nín xiǎng jì shénme?

I'd like to send a registered letter.
我想寄挂号信。Wǒ xiǎng jì guàhàoxìn.

①	②		③
Subjective 主体	Verbal 述谓		Objective 客体
	Mentality 心态	Action 行动	
you(polite) 您 [nín]	would like to 想 [xiǎng]		what 什么 [shénme]
			registered letter 挂号信 [guàhàoxìn]
		send 寄 [jì]	package 包裹 [bāoguǒ]
I 我 [wǒ]	want to 要 [yào]		express mail service 特快专递 [tèkuài zhāndì]
Sentence Making 造句 [zàojù]	What do you want to send? I want to send a package.		你要寄什么? 我要寄包裹。

Vocabulary 词语

平信 [píngxìn]	ordinary letter	汇款 [huìkuǎn]	remittance
航空信 [hángkōngxìn]	airmail	汇款单 [huìkuǎndān]	remittance sheet
挂号信 [guàhàoxìn]	registered letter	电子邮件 [diànzǐ yóujiàn]	e-mail
地址 [dìzhǐ]	address	电报 [diànbào]	telegram
发信人 [fāxìnrén]	sender; addresser	电话 [diànhuà]	telephone
收信人 [shōuxìnrén]	addressee	本市电话 [běnshì diànhuà]	local telephone
邮政编码 [yóuzhèng biānmǎ]	postal code	长途电话 [chángtú diànhuà]	long distance call
明信片 [míngxìnpiàn]	postcard	传真 [chuánzhēn]	fax
信纸 [xìnzhǐ]	letter paper	电话铃声 [diànhuà língshēng]	telephone ring
信封 [xìnfēng]	envelope	手机短信 [shǒujī duǎnxìn]	cell phone message
邮票 [yóupiào]	stamp	电话局 [diànhuàjú]	telephone exchange
邮筒 [yóutǒng]	mailbox	电话亭 [diànhuàtíng]	telephone kiosk
邮局 [yóujú]	post office	听筒 [tīngtǒng]	handset
特快专递 [tèkuài zhuāndì]	express mail service	分机 [fēnjī]	extension
包裹 [bāoguǒ]	package	占线 [zhànxiàn]	busy; engaged
印刷品 [yìnshuāpǐn]	printed matter	占线音 [zhànxiànyīn]	engaged tone

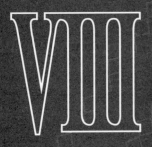

Studying and Working

学习和工作 [xuéxí hé gōngzuò]

071. Which department is your friend in? 你的朋友是哪个系的？

He is in the department of Computer Science. 他是计算机系的。

072. What course does Professor Li teach you this term? 李教授这学期教你们什么课？

Professor Li teaches us physics this term. 李教授这学期教我们物理学。

073. What did the guider explain to you just now? 解说员刚才给你们讲了什么？

The guider explained the historic site to us just now. 解说员刚才给我们讲了那个古迹。

074. Whom did Professor Liu persuade to go to university? 刘教授劝说谁上大学？

Professor Liu persuaded his son to go to university. 刘教授劝说儿子上大学。

075. Which university did you graduate from? 你是哪个大学毕业的？

I graduated from Beijing Language and Culture University. 我是北京语言大学毕业的。

076. What would you like to be in the future? 你将来想当什么样的人？

I'd like to be a scientist in the future. 我将来想当科学家。

077. Where do you work? 你在哪里工作？　　　　I work in a jewelry shop. 我在珠宝商店工作。

078. What does he do? 他是做什么的？　　　　He drives taxi. 他是开出租车的。

079. When did the Chairman of the Board appoint Doctor Cao Hui as the General Manager?
董事长什么时候任命了曹慧博士为总经理？

The Chairman of the Board appointed Doctor Cao Hui as the General Manager last Tuesday.
董事长上星期二任命了曹慧博士为总经理。

080. Why didn't Liu Fen go to work yesterday? 刘芬为什么昨天没上班？

Liu Fen didn't go to work yesterday because she was sick. 刘芬因为生病昨天没上班。

Which department is your friend in?
你的朋友是哪个系的？ Nǐ de péngyou shì nǎge xì de?

He is in the department of Computer Science.
他是计算机系的。 Tā shì jìsuànjī xì de.

① Subjective 主体		② Linking 联系	③ Relative 系体		
Determiner 限定	Person 人		Determiner 限定	Place 处所	Postpositive 后助词
your 你的 [nǐ de]	friend 朋友 [péngyou]	be 是 [shì]	which 哪个 [nǎge]	department 系 [xì]	{ } 的 [de]
her 她的 [tā de]	younger brother 弟弟 [dìdi]		computer science 计算机 [jìsuànjī]		
	you 你 [nǐ]		geology 地质 [dìzhì]		
	he 他 [tā]		foreign language 外语 [wàiyǔ]	college 学院 [xuéyuàn]	
Sentence Making 造句 [zàojù]	Which college are you in? I am in the school of Foreign Languages.		你是哪个学院的？ 我是外语学院的。		

Vocabulary　词语

哲学 [zhéxué]	philosophy	数学 [shùxué]	mathematics
文学 [wénxué]	literature	物理学 [wùlǐxué]	physics
语言学 [yǔyánxué]	linguistics	化学 [huàxué]	chemistry
逻辑学 [luójìxué]	logic	天文学 [tiānwénxué]	astronomy
历史学 [lìshǐxué]	history	地质学 [dìzhìxué]	geology
地理学 [dìlǐxué]	geography	计算机科学 [jìsuànjī kēxué]	computer science
考古学 [kǎogǔxué]	archaeology	信息工程 [xìnxī gōngchéng]	information engineering
艺术 [yìshù]	art	机械工程 [jīxiè gōngchéng]	mechanical engineering
美术 [měishù]	painting	建筑工程 [jiànzhù gōngchéng]	architectural engineering
音乐 [yīnyuè]	music	能源科学 [néngyuán kēxué]	science of energy sources
舞蹈 [wǔdǎo]	dance	管理科学 [guǎnlǐ kēxué]	administration science
戏剧 [xìjù]	drama	生命科学 [shēngmìng kēxué]	science of life
法学 [fǎxué]	law	生物工程 [shēngwù gōngchéng]	bioengineering
经济学 [jīngjìxué]	economics	医学 [yīxué]	medical science

李教授这学期教你们什么课？ Lǐ jiàoshòu zhè xuéqī jiāo nǐmen shénme kè?

Professor Li teaches us physics this term.
李教授这学期教我们物理学。 Lǐ jiàoshòu zhè xuéqī jiāo wǒmen wùlǐxué.

① Subjective 主体	② Time 时间	③ Action 行动	④ Dative 邻体	⑤ Objective 客体
Professor Li 李教授 [Lǐ jiàoshòu]	this term 这学期 [zhè xuéqī]		you(pl.) 你们 [nǐmen]	what course 什么课 [shénme kè]
				physics 物理学 [wùlǐxué]
Teacher Chen 陈老师 [Chén lǎoshī]		teach 教 [jiāo]	us 我们 [wǒmen]	philosophy 哲学 [zhéxué]
				grammar 语法学 [yǔfǎxué]
Doctor Liu 刘博士 [Liú bóshì]	last term 上学期 [shàng xuéqī]		graduate student 研究生 [yánjiūshēng]	literature 文学 [wénxué]

Sentence Making 造句 [zàojù]	What course did Professor Chen teach you last term? Professor Chen taught us literature last term.	陈教授上学期教你们什么课? 陈教授上学期教我们文学课。

Notes 注解

In Chinese, one of the "information transmitting" sentence frames is the "double-object sentence". In the frame, the predicative verb (information transmitting) takes two objects: the close object is dative (information receiver), the far object is objective (contents of information). For example, the verb "教 [jiāo](teach)" can take two objects (李教授教 我们物理学 Professor Li teaches us physics). But the verb "讲 [jiǎng] (explain)" cannot take two objects (* 李教授 讲我们物理学. Professor Li explains us physics). It should be expressed as "李教授给我们讲物理学 [Lǐ jiàoshòu gěi wǒmen jiǎng wùlǐxué]. (Professor Li explains physics to us.)". The usage of "讲 (explain)" is shown in detail on the next page. The information of some transmitting verbs which can take two objects similar to the verb "教 (teach)" is shown in the table on this page.

汉语"传递信息"的句式之一是"双宾语句"。这种句式"谓语动词 (信息传递)"的后边带两个"宾语"：近宾语是"邻体 (信息接收者)"，远宾语是"客体 (信息内容)"。如动词"教"可以带"双宾语"(李教授教我们物理学)。但动词"讲"不可带"双宾语"(* 李教授讲我们物理学)，只能说"李教授给我们讲物理学"。关于"讲"的用法详见下一页。本页的表中是一些类似于"教"那样可带"双宾语"的信息传递动词以及例句。

告诉 [gàosu]	tell	她告诉了她的丈夫一个秘密。 Tā gàosule tā de zhàngfu yí ge mìmì.	She told her husband a secret.
通知 [tōngzhī]	inform	他通知我他平安到达。 Tā tōngzhī wǒ tā píng'ān dàodá.	He informed me of his safe arrival.
转告 [zhuǎnggào]	pass on	我的朋友转告我一个消息。 wǒ de péngyou zhuǎnggào wǒ yí ge xiāoxī.	My friend passed on a message to me.

What did the guider explain to you just now?

解说员刚才给你们讲了什么？ Jiěshuōyuán gāngcái gěi nǐmen jiǎngle shénme?

The guider explained the historic site to us just now.

解说员刚才给我们讲了那个古迹。 Jiěshuōyuán gāngcái gěi wǒmen jiǎngle nàge gǔjì.

① Subjective 主体	② Time 时间	③ Beneficiary 涉体		④ Action 行动	⑤ Objective 客体
		Prepositive 前辅词	Substance 实体		
guider 解说员 [jiěshuōyuán]	just now 刚才 [gāngcái]	to 给 [gěi]	you(pl.) 你们 [nǐmen]	explain 讲了 [jiǎngle]	what 什么 [shénmen]
					historic site 那个古迹 [nàge gǔjì]
					story 一个故事 [yí ge gùshi]
grandpa 爷爷 [yéye]	yesterday 昨天 [zuótiān]		us 我们 [wǒmen]		history 中国历史 [Zhōngguó lìshǐ]
Sentence Making 造句 [zào jù]	What did your grandpa tell you yesterday? My grandpa told us a story yesterday.			爷爷昨天给你们讲了什么？ 爷爷昨天给我们讲了一个故事。	

Notes 注解

The second information transmitting sentence frame is a "single object sentence". In the frame, the predicative verb (information transmitting) takes only one object, i.e., "objective (information content)". The beneficiary (information receiver) is put before the predicative verb with a preposition "给 [gěi] (to)" or "向 [xiàng] (to)". The Chinese information transmitting verbs are shown in the table on this page.

汉语"传递信息"句式之二是"单宾语句"。这种句式"谓语动词（信息传递）"的后边只有一个"客体（信息内容）"。"谓语动词"的前边有一个带介词"给 (to)"或"向 (to)"的"涉体（信息获益者）"。本页的表是汉语"信息传递动词"。

Vocabulary 词语

讲 [jiǎng]	explain; say; relate	谈 [tán]	talk
讲解 [jiǎngjiě]	explain; explicate	解释 [jiěshì]	explain
讲授 [jiǎngshòu]	lecture; instruct	传达 [chuándá]	transmit; pass on
讲述 [jiǎngshù]	recount; relate	转达 [zhuǎndá]	pass on; convey
说 [shuō]	say	表达 [biǎodá]	express; indicate
述说 [shùshuō]	narrate	表白 [biǎobái]	explain oneself
诉说 [sùshuō]	narrate with feeling	表明 [biǎomíng]	demonstrate
解说 [jiěshuō]	explain	表示 [biǎoshì]	express; indicate
宣布 [xuānbù]	announce	显示 [xiǎnshì]	show; display

刘教授劝说谁上大学？ Liú jiàoshòu quànshuō shuí shàng dàxué?

Professor Liu persuaded his son to go to university.

刘教授劝说儿子上大学。 Liú jiàoshòu quànshuō érzi shàng dàxué.

①	②	③	④		
Subjective1 主体 1	Action1 行动 1	Dative1 邻体 1	Intention1 意图 1		
			Subjective2 主体 2	Action2 行动 2	Objective2 客体 2
Professor Liu 刘教授 [Liú jiàoshòu]	persuade 劝说 [quànshuō]	whom 谁 [shuí] son 儿子 [érzi]		go to 上 [shàng]	university 大学 [dàxué]
editor 编辑 [biānjí]	urge 催促 [cuīcù]	author 作者 [zuòzhě]		finish 完成 [wánchéng]	final text 定稿 [dìnggǎo]
army commander 军长 [jūnzhǎng]	order 命令 [mìnglìng]	which division 哪个师 [nǎge shī] the Third Division 第三师 [dì-sān shī]		put out 扑灭 [pūmiè]	forest fires 森林大火 [sēnlín dàhuǒ]
Sentence Making 造句 [zàojù]	Which Division did the Army Commander order to put out the forest fires? 军长命令哪个师扑灭森林大火？ The Army Commander ordered the Third Division to put out the forest fires. 军长命令第三师扑灭森林大火。				

Notes 注解

The third information transmitting sentence frame in Chinese is called the "pivotal sentence". In this sentence frame there is a "dative (information receiver)" after the predicative verb (information transmitting). The predicative verb has a function of "cause". It causes "the dative 1 (information receiver) to act as a "subjective 2 (intension achiever)" to achieve an "intention". The Chinese information transmitting verbs with "cause" function are shown in the table on this page.

汉语"传递信息"句式之三是"兼语句"。这种句式"谓语动词（信息传递）"的后边有一个"邻体（信息接收者）"。这个"谓语动词"具有"促使"的功能，它促使"邻体1（信息接收者）"同时兼任"主体2（意图实现者）"去实现一个"意图"。本页的表是汉语中具有"促使"功能的"信息传递动词"。

Vocabulary 词语

劝 [quàn]	persuade	劝说 [quànshuō]	persuade
催 [cuī]	urge	催促 [cuīcù]	urge
请 [qǐng]	invite; please	邀请 [yāoqǐng]	invite
叫 [jiào]	call	教唆 [jiàosuō]	incite; instigate
使 [shǐ]	use; make	唆使 [suōshǐ]	incite; abet sb. in
促使 [cùshǐ]	cause; impel	指使 [zhǐshǐ]	prompt; provoke
差使 [chāishǐ]	send; dispatch	迫使 [pòshǐ]	force
派 [pài]	appoint; assign	派遣 [pàiqiǎn]	dispatch; assign
令 [lìng]	order; command	命令 [mìnglìng]	order

Which university did you graduate from?

你是哪个大学毕业的？ Nǐ shì nǎge dàxué bìyè de?

I graduated from Beijing Language and Culture University.

我是北京语言大学毕业的。 Wǒ shì Běijīng Yǔyán Dàxué bìyè de.

① Subjective 主体	② Linking 联系	③ Relative 系体		
		Place 处所	Action 行动	Postpositive 后助词
you 你 [nǐ]		which university 哪个大学 [nǎge dàxué]		
I 我 [wǒ]	{be} 是 [shì]	Beijing Language and Culture University 北京语言大学 [Běijīng Yǔyán Dàxué]	graduate 毕业 [bìyè]	{ } 的 [de]
he 他 [tā]		Nanjing Normal University 南京师范大学 [Nánjīng Shīfàn Dàxué]		
Sentence Making 造句 [zàojù]	Which university did he graduate from? He graduated from Nanjing Normal University.		他是哪个大学毕业的？ 他是南京师范大学毕业的。	

Notes 注解

The radical "讠" is the changed form of "言 [yán] speech". It is called "言字旁 [yánzìpáng]". Sinograms with the radical "讠" all have meanings related to "语言 [yǔyán] (language)" or "说话 [shuōhuà] (to speak)".

字基(部首)"讠"是"言"字的变体，叫做"言字旁"。凡是"讠(言字旁)"的字都有"语言、说话"的意思。

Vocabulary 词语

言 [yán]	speech; say; word	读 [dú]	read
语 [yǔ]	words; speak; language	诵 [sòng]	read aloud; recite
语言 [yǔyán]	language	谈 [tán]	talk
说 [shuō]	speak; say	诉 [sù]	tell
话 [huà]	words	访 [fǎng]	visit
讨 [tǎo]	ask for; discuss	记 [jì]	remember; record; mark
论 [lùn]	theory; mention; comment	记忆 [jìyì]	remember; memory
讨论 [tǎolùn]	discuss	记录 [jìlù]	record
认 [rèn]	recognize; admit; accept	记号 [jìhào]	mark
识 [shí]	know; knowledge	诗 [shī]	poem
认识 [rènshi]	recognize; know; knowledge	谎话 [huǎnghuà]	lie

What would you like to be in the future?

你将来想当什么样的人？ Nǐ jiānglái xiǎng dāng shénme yàng de rén?

I'd like to be a scientist in the future.

我将来想当科学家。 Wǒ jiānglái xiǎng dāng kēxuéjiā.

① Subjective 主体	② Time 时间	③ Mentality 心态	④ Relative 系体
you 你 [nǐ]		would like to be 想当 [xiǎng dāng]	what kind of person 什么样的人 [shénme yàng de rén]
I 我 [wǒ]			scientist 科学家 [kēxuéjiā]
you(polite) 您 [nín]	in the future 将来 [jiānglái]		astronaut 宇航员 [yǔhángyuán]
he 他 [tā]			actor 演员 [yǎnyuán]
Wang Wei 王伟 [Wáng Wěi]		will become 要成为 [yào chéngwéi]	
Sentence Making 造句 [zàojù]	What will Wang Wei become in the future? Wang Wei will become an actor in the future.	王伟将来要成为什么样的人？ 王伟将来要成为一个演员。	

Notes 注解

In Chinese, those people with certain skills are called "××师 [shī]", and those people with greater achievements are called "××家 [jiā]".

汉语称有一定技能的人为 "××师"，称有较大成就的人为 "××家"。

Vocabulary 词语

技师 [jìshī]	senior technician	画家 [huàjiā]	painter
医师 [yīshī]	qualified doctor	作家 [zuòjiā]	writer
律师 [lǜshī]	lawyer	数学家 [shùxuéjiā]	mathematician
琴师 [qínshī]	fiddler; violinist	物理学家 [wùlǐxuéjiā]	physicist
建筑师 [jiànzhùshī]	architect	政治家 [zhèngzhìjiā]	politician
工程师 [gōngchéngshī]	engineer	哲学家 [zhéxuéjiā]	philosopher
机械师 [jīxièshī]	machinist	企业家 [qǐyèjiā]	entrepreneur
会计师 [kuàijìshī]	accountant	艺术家 [yìshùjiā]	artist
农艺师 [nóngyìshī]	agriculturist	作曲家 [zuòqǔjiā]	composer
园艺师 [yuányìshī]	horticulturist	外交家 [wàijiāojiā]	diplomat
魔术师 [móshùshī]	magician	思想家 [sīxiǎngjiā]	thinker

Where do you work?
你在哪里工作？ Nǐ zài nǎli gōngzuò?

I work in a jewelry shop.
我在珠宝商店工作。 Wǒ zài zhūbǎo shāngdiàn gōngzuò.

① Subjective 主体		② Location 地点	③ Action 行动
you 你 [nǐ]		where/which place 哪里 [nǎli]	work 工作 [gōngzuò]
I 我 [wǒ]	in 在 [zài]	jewelry shop 珠宝商店 [zhūbǎo shāngdiàn]	
he 他 [tā]		bank 银行 [yínháng]	work 上班 [shàngbān]
		hospital 医院 [yīyuàn]	
my brother 我弟弟 [wǒ dìdi]		Zhen Hua Computer Company 振华电脑公司 [Zhènhuá Diànnǎo Gōngsī]	practice 实习 [shíxí]
Sentence Making 造句 [zàojù]	Where does your brother work? My brother works in Zhen Hua Computer Company.		你弟弟在哪里上班？ 我弟弟在振华电脑公司上班。

Notes 注解

The radical "王" is the changed form of "玉 [yù] jade". It is called "玉字旁 [yùzìpáng]". Sinograms with "王（玉字旁）" and "玉（玉字底 [yùzìdǐ]）" all have meanings related to "玉石 [yùshí] jade or 珠宝 [zhūbǎo] treasure".

字基(部首)"王"是"玉"的变体，叫做"玉字旁"。凡是"王(玉字旁)"和"玉(玉字底)"的字都跟"玉石、珠宝"的意思有关。

Vocabulary 词语

玉 [yù]	jade	玉器 [yùqì]	jade artworks
宝 [bǎo]	treasure; precious	宝石 [bǎoshí]	precious stone
珠 [zhū]	bead; pearl	珠宝 [zhūbǎo]	treasure
珍 [zhēn]	treasure; valuable	珍珠 [xhēnzhū]	pearl
瑰 [guī]	jade-like stone; rare	瑰宝 [guībǎo]	rarity; gem
环 [huán]	ring; hoop	玉环 [yùhuán]	jade ring
玲 [líng]	tinkling of jade pieces	玲珑 [línglóng]	exquisite
瑞 [ruì]	one kind of jade artworks; lucky	玛瑙 [mǎnǎo]	agate
理 [lǐ]	texture (of jade); reason; deal with	珊瑚 [shānhú]	coral

What does he do?
他是做什么的？ Tā shì zuò shénme de?

078

He drives taxi.
他是开出租车的。 Tā shì kāi chūzūchē de.

① Subjective 主体	② Linking 联系	③ Relative 系体		
		Action 行动	Objective 客体	Postpositive 后助词
he 他 [tā]		do 做 [zuò]	what 什么 [shénme]	
		drive 开 [kāi]	taxi 出租车 [chūzūchē]	{ } 的 [de]
she 她 [tā]	{be} 是 [shì]	sell 卖 [mài]	ticket 票 [piào]	
		taxi driver 出租车司机 [chūzūchē sījī]		
he 我 [wǒ]		ticket seller 售票员 [shòupiàoyuán]		
Sentence Making 造句 [zàojù]	What does he do? He is a taxi driver.		他是做什么的？ 他是出租车司机。	

Notes 注解

In Chinese, the structure "action + objective + 的" can be used to indicate personal social status. However, this expression more or less has a manner of impoliteness. Therefore, in formal occasions, formal expression should be used. For instance, it is not polite if you say "他是送信的 (He is a person who sends letters)" instead of "他是邮递员 (He is a postman)".

汉语可以用"行动 + 客体 + 的"来表示人的"身份"。但是这种说法有或多或少不够尊重的语气，所以在正式的场合应该用正式的说法。例如把"他是邮递员"说成"他是送信的"就显得不够尊重。

Vocabulary 词语

开出租车的 [kāi chūzūchē de]	person who drives a taxi	出租车司机 [chūzūchē sījī]	taxi driver
演电影的 [yǎn diànyǐng de]	person who performs in a movie	电影演员 [diànyǐng yǎnyuán]	movie actor
送信的 [sòngxìn de]	person who sends letters	邮递员 [yóudìyuán]	postman
卖票的 [màipiào de]	person who sells tickets	售票员 [shòupiàoyuán]	ticket seller
喂猪的 [wèizhū de]	person who feeds pigs	饲养员 [sìyǎngyuán]	stockman
照相的 [zhàoxiàng de]	person who takes pictures	摄影师 [shèyǐngshī]	photographer
教书的 [jiāoshū de]	person who teaches students	教师 [jiàoshī]	teacher
做饭的 [zuòfàn de]	person who cooks food	厨师 [chúshī]	chef

When did the Chairman of the Board appoint Doctor Cao Hui as the General Manager?

董事长什么时候任命了曹慧博士为总经理？

Dǒngshìzhǎng shénme shíhou rènmìngle Cáo Huì bóshì wéi zǒngjīnglǐ?

The Chairman of the Board appointed Doctor Cao Hui as the General Manager last Tuesday.

董事长上星期二任命了曹慧博士为总经理。

Dǒngshìzhǎng shàng Xīngqī'èr rènmìngle Cáo Huì bóshì wéi zǒngjīnglǐ.

① Subjective 主体	② Time 时间	③ Action 行动	④ Objective 客体	⑤ Relative 系体	
				Prepositive 前辅词	Substance 实体
chairman of the board 董事长 [dǒngshìzhǎng]	when 什么时候 [shénme shíhou]	appoint 任命 [rènmìng]	Doctor Cao Hui 曹慧博士 [Cáo Huì bóshì]	as 为 [wéi]	general manager 总经理 [zǒngjīnglǐ]
minister 部长 [bùzhǎng]	last Tuesday 上星期二 [shàng Xīngqī'èr]	engage 聘任 [pìnrèn]	Engineer Lin 林工程师 [Lín gōngchéngshī]		general designer 总设计师 [zǒngshèjìshī]

Sentence Making 造句 [zàojù]	When did the Minister engage Engineer Lin as the General Designer? 部长什么时候聘任了林工程师为总设计师？ The Minister engaged Engineer Lin as the General Designer last Tuesday. 部长上星期二聘任林工程师为总设计师。

Notes 注解

In Chinese, if the objective and the relative are both put after the predicate verb, the objective is always put before the relative. This relative indicates the new position, social status, form of address or nickname of the objective. The verbs indicating new position and social status are the group of verbs such as "任命 [rènmìng] (appoint) and 拜认 [bàirèn] (acknowledge respectively as)". Prepositive "为 [wéi] (as)" should be added before the relative such as "拜他为师 [bài tā wéi shī] (acknowledge him as master-teacher)". The verbs indicating new address and nickname are the group of verbs as "叫 (call)". Prepositive "为 [wéi] (as)" is not necessary to be added before the relative such as "叫她母老虎 [jiào tā mǔlǎohǔ] (call her Tigress)". Verbs indicating new address or nickname and the examples are shown in the following table.

汉语"客体"和"系体"同时出现在"谓语动词"之后，总是"客体"在前，"系体"在后。这个"系体"表示的是"客体"新的"职务、身份、称呼、外号"等。表示新职务和身份的是"任命、拜认"类动词，在系体之前需要加介词"为"（拜他为师）。表示新称呼、外号的是"叫"类动词，在系体之前不必加介词"为"（叫她母老虎）。下列表中是表示新称呼和外号的动词及其例句。

叫 [jiào]	call	孩子们叫她阿姨。 Háizimen jiào tā āyí.	The children call her Aunt.
喊 [hǎn]	name	大家喊王慧活神仙。 Dàjiā hǎn Wáng Huì huóshénxiān.	People named Wang Hui Living Immortal.
称呼 [chēnghu]	address	我们称呼他博士。 Wǒmen chēnghu tā bóshì.	We address him as Doctor.

Why didn't Liu Fen go to work yesterday?
刘芬为什么昨天没上班？ Liú Fēn wèi shénme zuótiān méi shàngbān?

Liu Fen didn't go to work yesterday because she was sick.
刘芬因为生病昨天没上班。 Liú Fēn yīnwèi shēngbìng zuótiān méi shàngbān.

① Subjective 主体	② Causative 原由		③ Time 时间	④ Action 行动
Liu Fen 刘芬 [Liú Fēn]	why 为什么 [wèi shénme]		yesterday 昨天 [zuótiān]	go to work 上班 [shàngbān]
she 她 [tā]	for/because of 因为 [yīnwèi]	being sick 生病 [shēngbìng]	not 没 [méi]	go to school 上学 [shàngxué]
		having a fever 发烧 [fāshāo]		be on duty 值班 [zhíbān]
he 他 [tā]		having a headache 头疼 [tóuténg]	today 今天 [jīntiān]	attend the class 上课 [shàngkè]
Sentence Making 造句 [zàojù]	Why isn't she on duty today? She isn't on duty today because she has a fever.		她为什么今天没值班？ 她因为发烧今天没值班。	

Notes 注解

1. In a "basic sentence", the "causative" is always put in the second place in the sentence sequence. The contents of the "causative" mainly include "cause, reason, basis, and purpose".

2. The radical "疒" is called "病字头 [bìngzìtóu]". It is the top part of "病 (illness)". Sinograms with the radical "疒 (病字头)" all have meanings related to "病 (illness)".

1. 在"基础句"中，"原由"的顺序总是在第②位。"原由"的内容主要分为"原因、理由、依据、目的"。

2. 字基(部首)"疒"是"病"字的上头，叫"病字头"。凡是"疒(病字头)"的字都跟"病"的意思有关。

Vocabulary 词语

因 [yīn]	because of	病 [bìng]	ill; sick
因为 [yīnwèi]	because	症 [zhèng]	symptom
由于 [yóuyú]	owing to; thanks to	痛 [tòng]	pain; hurt
依据 [yījù]	in the light of	痒 [yǎng]	itch
按 [àn]	on the basis of	痰 [tán]	sputum (saliva and mucus)
按照 [ànzhào]	according to	疲 [pí]	tired
遵照 [zūnzhào]	in accordance with	疮 [chuāng]	sore
为 [wèi]	for	疤 [bā]	scar
为了 [wèile]	in order to	痕 [hén]	mark; trace
为着 [wèizhe]	for the sake of	癌 [ái]	cancer

Culture and Recreation

文化和娱乐 [wénhuà hé yúlè]

081. What do you usually do at weekend? 您在周末通常干什么？
　　　I usually watch movies at weekend. 我在周末通常看电影。
082. What kind of TV programs do you like? 你喜欢什么电视节目？
　　　I like TV series. 我喜欢电视连续剧。
083. What movie did Li Hua watch excitedly at the movie theater yesterday? 李华昨天在电影院激动地看了一部什么影片？
　　　Li Hua watched a science-fiction movie excitedly at the movie theater yesterday.
　　　李华昨天在电影院激动地看了一部科幻片。
084. What are the Chinese traditional festivals? 哪些是中国的传统节日？
　　　Spring festival is a traditional Chinese festival. 春节是中国的传统节日。
085. What are some scenic spots in Beijing? 哪些是北京的风景胜地？
　　　Summer Palace is a scenic spot in Beijing. 颐和园是北京的风景胜地。
086. What did Chen Hu give Li Fang at the evening party last weekend?
　　　陈虎上周末在晚会上送了李芳什么？
　　　Chen Hu gave Li Fang a bunch of red roses at the evening party last weekend.
　　　陈虎上周末在晚会上送了李芳一束红玫瑰。
087. What did the Minister award to her last week? 部长上周向她颁发了什么？
　　　The Minister awarded a gold medal to her last week. 部长上周向她颁发了金牌。
088. What animals are there in the zoo？动物园里有什么动物？
　　　There are lions in the zoo. 动物园里有狮子。
089. What rare birds are there in the zoo? 动物园里有什么珍禽？
　　　There are beautiful swans in the zoo. 动物园里有美丽的天鹅。
090. Where are there sharks? 哪里有鲨鱼？　　　　There are sharks in the aquarium. 水族馆里有鲨鱼。

What do you usually do at weekend?
您在周末通常干什么？ Nín zài zhōumò tōngcháng gàn shénme?

I usually watch movies at weekend.
我在周末通常看电影。 Wǒ zài zhōumò tōngcháng kàn diànyǐng.

① Subjective 主体	② Time 时间		③ Manner 方式	④ Action 行动	⑤ Objective 客体
	Prepositive 前辅词	Period 时期			
you 您 [nín]		weekend 周末 [zhōumò]	usually 通常 [tōngcháng]	do 干 [gàn]	what 什么 [shénme]
you 你 [nǐ]	on (at) 在 [zài]	Sunday 星期天 [Xīngqītiān]		watch 看 [kàn]	movie 电影 [diànyǐng]
I 我 [wǒ]		holiday 假日 [jiàrì]	often 往往 [wǎngwǎng]	attend 参加 [cānjiā]	concert 音乐会 [yīnyuèhuì]
Sentence Making 造句 [zàojù]	What do you often do on holidays? I often attend concerts on holidays.			你在假日往往干什么？ 我在假日往往参加音乐会。	

Vocabulary 词语

电影 [diànyǐng]	movie	音乐会 [yīnyuèhuì]	concert
电影院 [diànyǐngyuàn]	cinema	音乐厅 [yīnyuètīng]	concert hall
电影票 [diànyǐngpiào]	movie ticket	交响乐 [jiāoxiǎngyuè]	symphony
售票处 [shòupiàochù]	ticket office	管弦乐 [guǎnxiányuè]	orchestral music
放映厅 [fàngyìngtīng]	showing hall	摇滚乐 [yáogǔnyuè]	rock and roll
排 [pái]	row	轻音乐 [qīngyīnyuè]	light music
座位 [zuòwèi]	seat	歌剧 [gējù]	opera
休息厅 [xiūxitīng]	lobby; foyer	京剧 [jīngjù]	Beijing Opera
入口 [rùkǒu]	entrance	协奏曲 [xiézòuqǔ]	concerto
安全门 [ānquánmén]	exit	进行曲 [jìnxíngqǔ]	march
银幕 [yínmù]	screen	小夜曲 [xiǎoyèqǔ]	serenade
字幕 [zìmù]	caption; subtitle	圆舞曲 [yuánwǔqǔ]	waltz
宽银幕 [kuānyínmù]	wide-screen	流行歌曲 [liúxíng gēqǔ]	popular song

What kind of TV programs do you like?
你喜欢什么电视节目？ Nǐ xǐhuan shénme diànshì jiémù?

082

I like TV series.
我喜欢电视连续剧。Wǒ xǐhuan diànshì liánxùjù.

① Subjective 主体	② Mentality 心态	③ Relative 系体
you 你 [nǐ]		what kind of TV programs 什么电视节目 [shénme diànshì jiémù]
you(polite) 您 [nín]		TV series 电视连续剧 [diànshì liánxùjù]
I 我 [wǒ]	like 喜欢 [xǐhuan]	sports program 体育节目 [tǐyù jiémù]
he 他 [tā]		The Animal World 动物世界 [dòngwù shìjiè]
Li Li 李丽 [Lǐ Lì]		
Sentence Making 造句 [zàojù]	What kind of TV programs do you like? I like The Animal World.	你喜欢什么电视节目？ 我喜欢动物世界。

Notes 注解

In ancient China, the functions of "心 [xīn] (heart)" were defined as "思 [sī] (thought)" and "情 [qíng] (feelings)", so sinograms with the radical "心 (心字底 [xīnzìdǐ])" and "忄(情字旁 [qíngzìpáng])" both have meanings related to "思想 (thought)" or "情感 (feelings)".

古人认为"心"的功能是"思"和"情"，所以字基(部首)"心(心字底)"和"忄(情字旁)"所构成的字都跟"思想"和"情感"的意思有关。

Vocabulary 词语

心 [xīn]	heart; mind	情 [qíng]	feeling; love; situation
思 [sī]	thought	懂 [dǒng]	understand; know
想 [xiǎng]	thinking; would like to	惦 [diàn]	remember; think of
感 [gǎn]	feel; move; be grateful	悟 [wù]	realize; awaken
急 [jí]	urgent; worry; rapid	惊 [jīng]	start; be frightened
怒 [nù]	anger; forceful	恼 [nǎo]	displeased; furious
忍 [rěn]	stand; endure	惜 [xī]	value; cherish; treasure
怨 [yuàn]	hatred; resentment	恨 [hèn]	hate; be angry at
忘 [wàng]	forget	忆 [yì]	recall; recollect
愁 [chóu]	worry; sadness	忧 [yōu]	worry about

What movie did Li Hua watch excitedly at the movie theater yesterday?
李华昨天在电影院激动地看了一部什么影片？
Lǐ Huá zuótiān zài diànyǐngyuàn jīdòng de kànle yí bù shénme yǐngpiàn?

Li Hua watched a science-fiction movie excitedly at the movie theater yesterday.
李华昨天在电影院激动地看了一部科幻片。
Lǐ Huá zuótiān zài diànyǐngyuàn jīdòng de kànle yí bù kēhuànpiàn.

① Subjective 主体	② Time 时间	③ Location 地点	④ Manner 方式	⑤ Action 行动	⑥ Objective 客体	
					Amount 数量	Substance 实体
Li Hua 李华 [Lǐ Huá]	yesterday 昨天 [zuótiān]	at the movie theater 在电影院 [zài diànyǐngyuàn]	excitedly 激动地 [jīdòng de]	watch 看了 [kànle]	a 一部 [yí bù]	what movie 什么影片 [shénme yǐngpiàn] science-fiction movie 科幻片 [kēhuànpiàn]
old professor 老教授 [lǎo jiàoshòu]	Sunday 星期日 [Xīngqīrì]		leisurely 悠闲地 [yōuxián de]		two 两部 [liǎng bù]	art movie 艺术片 [yìshùpiàn]

Sentence Making 造句 [zàojù]
What two movies did the old professor watch leisurely at the movie theater on Sunday?
老教授星期日在电影院悠闲地看了两部什么影片？
The old professor leisurely watched two art movies at the movie theater on Sunday.
老教授星期日在电影院悠闲地看了两部艺术片。

Vocabulary   词语

故事片 [gùshìpiàn]	feature film	编剧 [biānjù]	script writer
科幻片 [kēhuànpiàn]	science-fiction movie	导演 [dǎoyǎn]	director
战争片 [zhànzhēngpiàn]	war movie	男演员 [nányǎnyuán]	actor
武打片 [wǔdǎpiàn]	martial arts movie	女演员 [nǚyǎnyuán]	actress
喜剧片 [xǐjùpiàn]	comedy	主角 [zhǔjué]	leading actor
悲剧片 [bēijùpiàn]	tragedy	配角 [pèijué]	supporting role
爱情片 [àiqíngpiàn]	love/romantic movie	电影明星 [diànyǐng míngxīng]	movie star
艺术片 [yìshùpiàn]	art movie	摄影师 [shèyǐngshī]	camera man
动画片 [dònghuàpiàn]	cartoon film	化妆师 [huàzhuāngshī]	makeup man
恐怖片 [kǒngbùpiàn]	horror movie	道具师 [dàojùshī]	property master
音乐片 [yīnyuèpiàn]	musical film	录音师 [lùyīnshī]	recordist
侦探片 [zhēntànpiàn]	detective film	灯光师 [dēngguāngshī]	lighting engineer
新闻片 [xīnwénpiàn]	newsreel	布景师 [bùjǐngshī]	set designer
纪录片 [jìlùpiàn]	documentary	剪辑师 [jiǎnjíshī]	film cutter

Spring Festival is a traditional Chinese festival.
春节是中国的传统节日。 Chūn Jié shì Zhōngguó de chuántǒng jiérì.

	①	②	③		
	Subjective 主体	Linking 联系	Relative 系体		
			Determiner 限定	Category 类别	Substance 实体
	what 哪些 [nǎxiē] Spring Festival 春节 [Chūn Jié] Dragon Boat Festival 端午节 [Duānwǔ Jié] Mid-autumn Festival 中秋节 [Zhōngqiū Jié]	is 是 [shì]	Chinese 中国的 [Zhōngguó de]	traditional 传统 [chuántǒng]	festival 节日 [jiérì]
Sentence Making 造句 [zàojù]	What are the Chinese traditional festivals? Mid-autumn festival is a traditional Chinese festival.		哪些是中国的传统节日？ 中秋节是中国的传统节日。		

Notes 注解

The dates of Chinese traditional festivals are based on the dates of the Chinese lunar calendar. In the lunar calendar, one month is about the period that it takes the moon to make one circle around the earth, so the moon is the roundest on the fifteenth every month. Some references to Chinese traditional festivals are shown in the following table.

中国传统节日的日期都是"阴历年"(lunar year) 的日期。阴历年的一个月大约是月亮绕地球一圈的周期，所以阴历年每月十五的月亮都是最圆的。下列的表中是有关中国传统节日的一些资料。

节日 [jiérì]	Festival	日期 [rìqī]	Date	食品 [shípǐn]	Food	活动 [huódòng]	Activity
春节 [Chūn Jié]	Spring Festival	阴历一月初一 [yīnlì Yīyuè chū yī]	1st day of the first lunar month	饺子 [jiǎozi]	dumpling	团聚 [tuánjù]	family reunion
元宵节 [Yuánxiāo Jié]	Lantern Festival	阴历一月十五 [yīnlì Yīyuè shíwǔ]	15th day of the first lunar month	元宵 [yuánxiāo]	glutinous rice ball	观灯 [guān dēng]	enjoying lanterns
端午节 [Duānwǔ Jié]	Dragon Boat Festival	阴历五月初五 [yīnlì Wǔyuè chū wǔ]	5th day of the fifth lunar month	粽子 [zòngzi]	rice dumpling wrapped in reed leaves	赛龙舟 [sài lóngzhōu]	dragon boat racing
中秋节 [Zhōngqiū Jié]	Mid-Autumn Festival	阴历八月十五 [yīnlì Bāyuè shíwǔ]	15th day of the eighth lunar month	月饼 [yuèbing]	moon cake	赏月 [shǎng yuè]	enjoying the full moon

What are some scenic spots in Beijing?
哪些是北京的风景胜地？ Nǎxiē shì Běijīng de fēngjǐng shèngdì?

Summer Palace is a scenic spot in Beijing.
颐和园是北京的风景胜地。 Yíhéyuán shì Běijīng de fēngjǐng shèngdì.

① Subjective 主体	② Linking 联系	③ Relative 系体		
		Determiner 限定	Category 类别	Substance 实体
what 哪些 [nǎxiē]			scenic 风景 [fēngjǐng]	spots 胜地 [shèngdì]
Summer Palace 颐和园 [Yíhéyuán]	is/are 是 [shì]	Beijing's 北京的 [Běijīng de]		
Palace Museum 故宫博物院 [Gùgōng Bówùyuàn]				
the Great Wall 长城 [Chángchéng]			historic 历史 [lìshǐ]	historic sites 古迹 [gǔjì]
Sentence Making 造句 [zàojù]	What are some historic sites in Beijing? The Great Wall is a historic site in Beijing.		哪些是北京的历史古迹？ 长城是北京的历史古迹。	

Vocabulary 词语

天安门广场 [Tiān'ānmén Guǎngchǎng]	Tian'anmen Square
故宫博物院 [Gùgōng Bówùyuàn]	Palace Museum
中国历史博物馆 [Zhōngguó Lìshǐ Bówùguǎn]	Museum of the Chinese History
中国革命博物馆 [Zhōngguó Gémìng Bówùguǎn]	Museum of the Chinese Revolution
中国国家博物馆 [Zhōngguó Guójiā Bówùguǎn]	The National Museum of China
天坛 [Tiāntán]	the Temple of Heaven
白塔寺 [Báitǎsì]	the Temple of the White Pagoda
北海公园 [Běihǎi Gōngyuán]	Beihai Park
八达岭长城 [Bādálǐng Chángchéng]	the Great Wall at Badaling
明十三陵 [Míng Shísānlíng]	Ming Tombs
颐和园 [Yíhéyuán]	Summer Palace
北京植物园 [Běijīng Zhíwùyuán]	Beijing Botanical Garden
北京动物园 [Běijīng Dòngwùyuán]	Beijing Zoo
北京天文馆 [Běijīng Tiānwénguǎn]	Beijing Planetarium

What did Chen Hu give Li Fang at the evening party last weekend?
陈虎上周末在晚会上送了李芳什么？

Chén Hǔ shàng zhōumò zài wǎnhuì shang sòngle Lǐ Fāng shénme?

Chen Hu gave Li Fang a bunch of red roses at the evening party last weekend.
陈虎上周末在晚会上送了李芳一束红玫瑰。

Chén Hǔ shàng zhōumò zài wǎnhuì shang sòngle Lǐ Fāng yí shù hóng méigui.

① Subjective 主体	② Time 时间	③ Location 地点	④ Verbal 述谓 Action 行动	Postpositive 后助词	⑤ Dative 邻体	⑥ Objective 客体
Chen Hu 陈虎 [Chén Hǔ]	last weekend 上周末 [shàng zhōumò]	at the party 在晚会上 [zài wǎnhuì shang]			Li Fang 李芳 [Lǐ Fāng]	what 什么 [shénme]
Li Qiang 李强 [Lǐ Qiáng]	last month 上个月 [shàng ge yuè]	in the park 在公园 [zài gōngyuán]	give 送 [sòng]	{了} [le]	Wang Li 王莉 [Wáng Lì]	a bunch of red roses 一束红玫瑰 [yí shù hóng méigui]
he 他 [tā]	yesterday 昨天 [zuótiān]	in the theatre 在剧院 [zài jùyuàn]			her 她 [tā]	a box of chocolates 一盒巧克力 [yì hé qiǎokèlì]
Sentence Making 造句 [zàojù]	What did he give her in the theatre yesterday? He gave her a box of chocolates in the theatre yesterday.				他昨天在剧院送了她什么？ 他昨天在剧院送了她一盒巧克力。	

Notes 注解

One of the "ownership transferring" sentence frames is the "double object sentence". In the frame, the predicative verb (ownership transferring) takes two objects: the close object is dative (ownership receiver), and the far object is objective (ownership). For example, the verb "赠送 (give)" can take two objects (陈虎赠送李芳一束玫瑰 . Chen Hu gave Li Fang a bunch of roses). However the verb "颁发 (award)" cannot take two objects (* 大会主席颁发她金牌 . The chairman of the meeting awarded her a gold medal). It should be expressed as "大会主席向她颁发金牌 . (The chairman of the meeting awarded a gold medal to her)". The usage of "颁发 (award)" is shown in detail on next page. The information of some ownership transferring verbs which can take two objects, similar to the verb "送 (give)", is shown in the table on this page.

汉语"物权转移"的句式之一是"双宾语句"。这种句式"谓语动词（物权转移）"的后边带两个"宾语"：近宾语是"邻体（物权接收者）"，远宾语是"客体（物权）"。如动词"赠送"可以带"双宾语"（陈虎赠送李芳一束玫瑰）。但动词"颁发"不可带双宾语（*大会主席颁发她金牌），只能说"大会主席向她颁发金牌"。关于"颁发"的用法详见下一页。本页的表中是一些类似于"送"那样可带"双宾语"的物权转移动词以及例句。

献给 [xiàngěi]	present	她献给英雄一面锦旗。 Tā xiàn gěi yīngxióng yí miàn jǐngqí.	She presented the hero a silk banner.
赏 [shǎng]	reward	他赏那个男孩儿十块钱。 Tā shǎng nàge nánháir shí kuài qián.	He rewarded the boy with 10 yuan.
赠送 [zèngsòng]	give	我的朋友赠送我一本字典。 wǒ de péngyou zèngsòng wǒ yì běn zìdiǎn.	My friend gave me a dictionary.

What did the Minister award to her last week?
部长上周向她颁发了什么？ Bùzhǎng shàngzhōu xiàng tā bānfāle shénme?

The Minister awarded a gold medal to her last week.
部长上周向她颁发了金牌。 Bùzhǎng shàngzhōu xiàng tā bānfāle jīnpái.

① Subjective 主体	② Time 时间	③ Beneficiary 涉体		④ Action 行动	⑤ Objective 客体
		Prepositive 前辅词	Substance 实体		
Minister 部长 [bùzhǎng]	last week 上周 [shàngzhōu]	to 向 [xiàng]	her 她 [tā]	award 颁发了 [bānfā le]	what 什么 [shénme]
			you(pl.) 你们 [nǐmen]		gold medal 金牌 [jīnpái]
					citation 奖状 [jiǎngzhuàng]
Mayor 市长 [shìzhǎng]	on June 8th 6月8日 [Liùyuè bārì]		us 我们 [wǒmen]	issue 发了 [fā le]	silk banner 锦旗 [jǐnqí]
Sentence Making 造句 [zàojù]	What did the Mayor issue to you on June 8th? The Mayor issued a citation to us on June 8th.			市长6月8日向你们发了什么？ 市长6月8日向我们发了奖状。	

Notes 注解

The second "ownership transferring" sentence frame is the "single object sentence". In the frame, the predicative verb (ownership transferring) takes only one object, i.e., "objective (ownership)". The "beneficiary (ownership receiver)" is put before the predicative verb with a preposition word "向 (to)". The "ownership transferring verbs" are shown in the table on this page.

汉语"物权转移"句式之二是"单宾语句"。这种句式"谓语动词(物权转移)"之后只有一个"客体(物权)"。谓语动词之前有一个带前辅词"向(to)"的"涉体(物权获益者)"。本页的表中是这种"物权转移动词"。

Vocabulary 词语

颁 [bān]	issue; promulgate	征 [zhēng]	call up; collect; solicit
颁发 [bānfā]	award; issue	征收 [zhēngshōu]	levy; collect; impose
发 [fā]	send out; shoot; show	征求 [zhēngqiú]	solicit; seek for; ask for
发放 [fāfàng]	provide; issue	摊 [tān]	lay out; booth; share
发送 [fāsòng]	dispatch; send out	摊派 [tānpài]	apportion
分发 [fēnfā]	distribute; hand out	分摊 [fēntān]	share; apportion
捐 [juān]	donate; abnegate; levy	索要 [suǒyào]	extort
捐赠 [juānzèng]	donate; contribute	索取 [suǒqǔ]	ask for; demand
献 [xiàn]	dedicate; show	勒索 [lèsuǒ]	extort
奉献 [fèngxiàn]	devote; dedicate	敲诈 [qiāozhà]	blackmail

What animals are there in the zoo?

动物园里有什么动物？ Dòngwùyuán li yǒu shénme dòngwù?

There are lions in the zoo.

动物园里有狮子。Dòngwùyuán li yǒu shīzi.

①		②	③
Location 地点		Existing 存在	Subjective 主体
Place 处所	Postpositive 后助词		
zoo 动物园 [dòngwùyuán]	in {里 [li]}	there be (is/are) {有 [yǒu]}	what animal 什么动物 [shénme dòngwù]
			lion 狮子 [shīzi]
			monkey 猴子 [hóuzi]
circus 马戏团 [mǎxìtuán]			elephant 大象 [dàxiàng]
Sentence Making 造句 [zàojù]	What animals are there in the circus? There are elephants in the circus.		马戏团里有什么动物？ 马戏团里有大象。

Notes 注解

1. The radical "犭" is called "狗字旁 [gǒuzìpáng]". It is the left part of "狗 [gǒu] (dog)". Sinograms with the radical "犭" have meanings related to "dog, beast or animal".

2. Sinograms with the radical "马 [mǎ] (horse)" all have meanings related to "horse or other animals with great strength like horse".

1. 字基(部首) "犭" 是 "狗" 的左偏旁，叫做 "狗字旁"。凡是 "犭(狗字旁)" 的字都跟 "狗、兽、动物" 的意思有关。

2. 字基(部首)是 "马" 的字都跟 "马和类似于马的大力畜" 的意思有关。

Vocabulary 词语

狗 [gǒu]	dog	马 [mǎ]	horse
猫 [māo]	cat	驴 [lú]	donkey
狼 [láng]	wolf	骡 [luó]	mule
狐狸 [húli]	fox	骆驼 [luòtuo]	camel
狮子 [shīzi]	lion	骑 [qí]	ride
猴子 [hóuzi]	monkey	驯 [xùn]	tame
猿 [yuán]	ape	驶 [shǐ]	drive
猩猩 [xīngxing]	chimpanzee	驰 [chí]	gallop
猪 [zhū]	pig	驮 [tuó]	carry on the back of a horse

What rare birds are there in the zoo?
动物园里有什么珍禽？ Dòngwùyuán li yǒu shénme zhēnqín?

There are beautiful swans in the zoo.
动物园里有美丽的天鹅。 Dòngwùyuán li yǒu měilì de tiān'é.

Location 地点		Existing 存在	Subjective 主体	
Place 处所	Postpositive 后助词		Attribute 属性	Substance 实物
zoo 动物园 [dòngwùyuán]	in {里 [li]}	there be (is/are) {有 [yǒu]}	what rare bird 什么珍禽 [shénme zhēnqín]	
			beautiful 美丽的 [měilì de]	swan 天鹅 [tiān'é]
			graceful 优雅的 [yōuyǎ de]	parrot 鹦鹉 [yīngwǔ]
			lovely 可爱的 [kě'ài de]	peacock 孔雀 [kǒngquè]
Sentence Making 造句 [zàojù]	What rare birds are there in the zoo? There are lovely peacocks in the zoo.		动物园里有什么珍禽？ 动物园里有可爱的孔雀。	

Notes 注解

Sinograms with the radical "鸟 [niǎo] (bird)" all have meanings related to "birds".
字基(部首)是"鸟"的字都跟"鸟类"的意思有关。

Vocabulary 词语

鸟 [niǎo]	bird	鹦鹉 [yīngwǔ]	parrot
鸡 [jī]	chicken	鸳鸯 [yuānyāng]	mandarin duck
鸭 [yā]	duck	鹌鹑 [ānchún]	quail
鹅 [é]	goose	斑鸠 [bānjiū]	turtledove
鹏 [péng]	roc (mythical bird)	乌鸦 [wūyā]	crow
鹤 [hè]	crane	喜鹊 [xǐquè]	magpie
鹭 [lù]	heron	黄莺 [huángyīng]	oriole
鸽子 [gēzi]	pigeon	杜鹃 [dùjuān]	cuckoo
鹞子 [yàozi]	sparrow	秃鹫 [tūjiù]	vulture
鸵鸟 [tuóniǎo]	ostrich	鸣 [míng]	chirp

Where are there sharks?
哪里有鲨鱼？ Nǎli yǒu shāyú?

There are sharks in the aquarium.
水族馆里有鲨鱼。 Shuǐzúguǎn li yǒu shāyú.

① Location 地点		② Existing 存在	③ Subjective 主体
Place 处所	Postpositive 后助词		
where 哪里 [nǎli]			shark 鲨鱼 [shāyú]
aquarium 水族馆 [shuǐzúguǎn]		there be (is/are) 有 [yǒu]	crocodile 鳄鱼 [èyú]
	in {里 [li]}		seal 海豹 [hǎibào]
sea 大海 [dà hǎi]			sea lion 海狮 [hǎishī]
Sentence Making 造句 [zàojù]	Where are there seals? There are seals in the sea.		哪里有海豹？ 大海里有海豹。

Notes 注解

1. Sinograms with the radical "鱼 [yú] fish " all have meanings related to "water animal in the shape of a fish".
2. Sinograms with the radical "虫 [chóng] worm " all have meanings related to "insect" or "reptile".
1. 字基(部首)是"鱼"的字都有"外形像鱼的水生动物"的意思。
2. 字基(部首)是"虫"的字都有"昆虫或爬虫"的意思。

Vocabulary 词语

鱼 [yú]	fish	虫 [chóng]	worm
鳞 [lín]	scale	蛇 [shé]	snake
鳍 [qí]	fin	蛙 [wā]	frog
鳄鱼 [èyú]	crocodile	蝉 [chán]	cicada
鲸鱼 [jīngyú]	whale	蚊子 [wénzi]	mosquito
鲤鱼 [lǐyú]	carp	苍蝇 [cāngyíng]	fly
鲫鱼 [jìyú]	crucial carp	蚂蚁 [mǎyǐ]	ant
鳝鱼 [shànyú]	eel	蝴蝶 [húdié]	butterfly
鲨鱼 [shāyú]	shark	蜻蜓 [qīngtíng]	dragonfly

Sports and Health

体育和卫生 [Tǐyù hé wèishēng]

091. What kind of sports do you like? 你喜欢什么运动？ I like football. 我喜欢足球。

092. What game is there this evening? 今天晚上有什么比赛？

There is track and field trial match this evening. 今天晚上有田径预赛。

093. How long did she play tennis today? 她今天打网球打了多长时间？

She played tennis for three hours today. 她今天打网球打了三个小时。

094. What stadiums are there in Beijing? 北京有哪些体育馆？

There is the National Stadium in Beijing. 北京有国家体育馆。

095. When is the semifinal of women's tennis scheduled? 女子网球半决赛定在什么时候？

The semifinal of women's tennis is scheduled at eight o'clock tomorrow evening.
女子网球半决赛定在明天晚上八点。

096. What symptoms do you have? 你哪里不舒服？ I have a stomachache. 我肚子疼。

097. What disease is he suffering from? 他有什么病？ He is suffering from heart disease. 他有心脏病。

098. What departments are there in this hospital? 这个医院有哪些科室？

There is a surgical department in this hospital. 这个医院有外科。

099. What symptoms of the patient did the nurse check? 护士检查了病人的哪些方面？

The nurse checked the patient's temperature. 护士量了病人的体温。

100. What medicine did the doctor prescribe for the patient? 医生给病人开了什么药？

The doctor prescribed traditional Chinese medicine for the patient. 医生给病人开了中药。

What kind of sports do you like?
你喜欢什么运动？ Nǐ xǐhuan shénme yùndòng?

I like football.
我喜欢足球。 Wǒ xǐhuan zúqiú.

① Subjective 主体	② Mentality 心态	③ Objective 客体
you 你 [nǐ]		what kinds of sports 什么运动 [shénme yùndòng]
I 我 [wǒ]	like 喜欢 [xǐhuan]	football/soccer 足球 [zúqiú]
he 他 [tā]		basketball 篮球 [lánqiú]
Wang Xiang 王祥 [Wáng Xiáng]		swimming 游泳 [yóuyǒng]
Sentence Making 造句 [zàojù]	What kind of sports does Wang Xiang like? He likes swimming.	王祥喜欢什么运动？ 他喜欢游泳。

Vocabulary 词语

体育 [tǐyù]	sports	中国式摔跤 [Zhōngguóshì shuāijiāo]	Chinese style wrestling
体操 [tǐcāo]	gymnastics	自由式摔跤 [zìyóushì shuāijiāo]	freestyle wrestling
水球 [shuǐqiú]	water polo	跆拳道 [táiquándào]	tae kwon do
跳水 [tiàoshuǐ]	diving	柔道 [róudào]	judo
冲浪 [chōnglàng]	surfing	空手道 [kōngshǒudào]	karate
帆船 [fānchuán]	sailing	拳击 [quánjī]	boxing
划船 [huáchuán]	boat racing	击剑 [jījiàn]	fencing
举重 [jǔzhòng]	weight lifting	自行车比赛 [zìxíngchē bǐsài]	bicycle racing
挺举 [tǐngjǔ]	clean and jerk	汽车越野赛 [qìchē yuèyěsài]	cross-country motor racing
抓举 [zhuājǔ]	snatch	汽车拉力赛 [qìchē lālìsài]	rally
冰球 [bīngqiú]	ice hockey	气手枪射击 [qìshǒuqiāng shèjī]	air pistol shooting
滑冰 [huábīng]	skating	气步枪射击 [qìbùqiāng shèjī]	air rifle shooting
滑雪 [huáxuě]	skiing	飞靶射击 [fēibǎ shèjī]	trap-shooting

What game is there this evening?
今天晚上有什么比赛？ Jīntiān wǎnshang yǒu shénme bǐsài?

There is track and field trial match this evening.
今天晚上有田径预赛。 Jīntiān wǎnshang yǒu tiánjìng yùsài.

① Time 时间		② Existing 存在	③ Subjective 主体	
			Determiner 限定	Substance 实体
today/this 今天 [jīntiān]	evening 晚上 [wǎnshang]		what 什么 [shénme]	game 比赛 [bǐsài]
			basketball 篮球 [lánqiú]	trial match 预赛 [yùsài]
tomorrow 明天 [míngtiān]		there be (is/are) 有 [yǒu]	track and field 田径 [tiánjìng]	semifinal 复赛 [fùsài]
			swimming 游泳 [yóuyǒng]	
Saturday 星期六 [Xīngqīliù]	afternoon 下午 [xiàwǔ]		springboard diving 跳板跳水 [tiàobǎntiàoshuǐ]	final 决赛 [juésài]
Sentence Making 造句 [zàojù]	What games are there tomorrow afternoon? There is a basketball final tomorrow afternoon.		明天下午有什么比赛？ 明天下午有篮球决赛。	

Notes   注解

1. The radical "⊞" is called "田字旁 [tiánzìpáng]". It is the changed form of "田 [tián] (field)". Sinograms with radical "⊞ (田字旁)" all have meanings related to "田地 [tiándì] (field)".

2. The radical "彳" is called "径字旁 [jìngzìpáng]". It is the left part of "径 [jìng] (road)". Sinograms with the radical "彳 (径字旁)" all have meanings related to "路径 [lùjìng] (road)" or "行走 [xíngzǒu] (walk)".

1. 字基(部首) "⊞" 是 "田" 字的变体，叫 "田字旁"。凡是 "⊞ (田字旁)" 的字都跟 "田地" 的意思有关。

2. 字基(部首) "彳" 是 "径" 字的左旁，叫 "径字旁"。凡是 "彳 (径字旁)" 的字都跟 "路径、行走" 的意思有关。

Vocabulary   词语

田 [tián]	field	径 [jìng]	road; way; track
畦 [wā]	farm plot	行 [xíng]	walk; travel
畔 [pàn]	border of a field; side	征 [zhēng]	march
稻田 [dàotián]	rice field	往 [wǎng]	go; towards; past
梯田 [tītián]	terraced field	街 [jiē]	street
油田 [yóutián]	oil field	上街 [shàngjiē]	go shopping
田坎 [tiánkǎn]	ridge	逛街 [guàngjiē]	take a stroll in the street
田鼠 [tiánshǔ]	field vole	途径 [tújìng]	way; road; approach
田赛 [tiánsài]	field events	径赛 [jìngsài]	track events

How long did she play tennis today?
她今天打网球打了多长时间？ Tā jīntiān dǎ wǎngqiú dǎle duōcháng shíjiān?

She played tennis for three hours today.
她今天打网球打了三个小时。 Tā jīntiān dǎ wǎngqiú dǎle sān gè xiǎoshí.

① Subjective 主体	② Time 时间	③ Verbal 述谓 Action 行动	④ Objective 客体	⑤ Verbal 述谓 Action 行动	⑤ Verbal 述谓 Postpositive 后助词	⑥ Duration 时量
she 她 [tā]	today 今天 [jīntiān]	play 打 [dǎ]	tennis 网球 [wǎngqiú]	play 打 [dǎ]		how long 多长时间 [duōcháng shíjiān]
he 他 [tā]	yesterday 昨天 [zuótiān]		basketball 篮球 [lánqiú]		{ } 了 [le]	three hours 三个小时 [sān gè xiǎoshí]
Li Xing 李兴 [Lǐ Xīng]		play 踢 [tī]	football 足球 [zúqiú]	play 踢 [tī]		for a long time 很久 [hěnjiǔ]

Sentence Making 造句 [zàojù]	How long did Li Xing play football yesterday? 李兴昨天踢足球踢了多长时间？ He played football for a long time yesterday. 他昨天踢足球踢了很久。

Notes 注解

"Play a ball game" can not all be translated from English to Chinese as "打球 [dǎqiú]". Sinograms indicating action are classified according to the parts of the human body which make the action. Sinograms indicating actions with "hands" all use the radical "扌(手字旁 [shǒuzìpáng] hand)"; actions with "feet" all use the radical "足(足字旁 [zúzìpáng] foot)". We play basketball with our hands, we should translate "play basketball" into "打篮球 [dǎ liánqiú]". On the other hand, we play football with our feet, so we should translate "play football" into "踢足球 [tī zúqiú]".

英语 "play a ball game" 不能一律译为汉语 "打球"。汉语表示动作的字是按动作所用部位来分类的。用 "手" 的动作的字都有 "扌(手字旁)"；用 "足" 的动作的字都有 "足(足字旁)"。用 "手" 的 "play basketball" 是 "打篮球"，而用 "足" 的 "play football" 是 "踢足球"。

Vocabulary 词语

手 [shǒu]	hand	足 [zú]	foot
打 [dǎ]	beat; hit	踢 [tī]	kick
推 [tuī]	push; postpone	跑 [pǎo]	run
拉 [lā]	pull	跳 [tiào]	jump
抱 [bào]	embrace; hug	踏 [tà]	tread
提 [tí]	carry	踩 [cǎi]	trample
摘 [zhāi]	pick	跺 [duò]	stamp

What stadiums are there in Beijing?
北京有哪些体育馆？ Běijīng yǒu nǎxiē tǐyùguǎn?

There is the National Stadium in Beijing.
北京有国家体育馆。 Běijīng yǒu Guójiā Tǐyùguǎn.

① Location 地点	② Existing 存在	③ Subjective 主体
Beijing 北京 [Běijīng]	there be (is/are) 有 [yǒu]	what stadium 哪些体育馆 [nǎxiē tǐyùguǎn] National Stadium 国家体育馆 [Guójiā Tǐyùguǎn] Olympic Sports Center Stadium 奥体中心体育馆 [Àotǐ Zhōngxīn Tǐyùguǎn] Worker's Stadium 工人体育馆 [Gōngrén Tǐyùguǎn]
Sentence Making 造句 [zàojù]	What stadium are there in Beijing? There is the Worker's Stadium in Beijing.	北京有哪些体育馆？ 北京有工人体育馆。

Vocabulary 词语

体育馆 [tǐyùguǎn]	gymnasium	健身房 [jiànshēnfáng]	fitness center
体育场 [tǐyùchǎng]	stadium	健身卡 [jiànshēnkǎ]	fitness card
室内运动 [shìnèi yùndòng]	indoor sports	哑铃 [yǎlíng]	dumbbell
室外运动 [shìwài yùndòng]	outdoor sports	杠铃 [gànglíng]	barbell
跳高 [tiàogāo]	high jump	单杠 [dāngàng]	horizontal bar
跳远 [tiàoyuǎn]	long jump	双杠 [shuānggàng]	parallel bars
三级跳远 [sānjí tiàoyuǎn]	triple-jump	高低杠 [gāodīgàng]	high–low bars
撑杆跳高 [chēnggān tiàogāo]	pole-jump	吊环 [diàohuán]	hand rings
跨栏 [kuàlán]	hurdle race	鞍马 [ānmǎ]	pommel horse
掷铁饼 [zhì tiěbǐng]	discus	跳箱 [tiàoxiāng]	vaulting box
掷铅球 [zhì qiānqiú]	shot-put	跳马 [tiàomǎ]	vaulting horse
掷链球 [zhì liànqiú]	hammer-throw	自由体操 [zìyóu tǐcāo]	free exercises
掷标枪 [zhì biāoqiāng]	javelin	器械体操 [qìxiè tǐcāo]	gymnastic on apparatus
马拉松 [mǎlāsōng]	marathon	团体操 [tuántǐcāo]	group exercises
竞走 [jìngzǒu]	speed-walking	广播操 [guǎngbōcāo]	broadcast calisthenics

When is the semifinal of women's tennis scheduled?
女子网球半决赛定在什么时候? Nǚzǐ wǎngqiú bànjuésài dìng zài shénme shíhou?

The semifinal of women's tennis is scheduled at eight o'clock tomorrow evening.
女子网球半决赛定在明天晚上八点。 Nǚzǐ wǎngqiú bànjuésài dìng zài míngtiān wǎnshang bā diǎn.

① Subjective 主体		② Linking 联系	③ Time 时间			
women's tennis 女子网球 [nǚzǐ wǎngqiú]	semifinal 半决赛 [bànjuésài]		when 什么时候 [shénme shíhou]			
men's basketball 男子篮球 [nánzǐ lánqiú]		be scheduled 定在 [dìngzài]	tomorrow 明天 [míngtiān]			eight o'clock 八点 [bā diǎn]
women's volleyball 女子排球 [nǚzǐ páiqiú]	final 决赛 [juésài]		Sunday 星期天 [Xīngqītiān]	evening 晚上 [wǎnshang]		half past seven 七点半 [qī diǎn bàn]
Sentence Making 造句 [zàojù]	When is the final of women's volleyball scheduled? 女子排球决赛定在什么时候? The final of women's volleyball is scheduled at 7:30 on Sunday evening. 女子排球决赛定在星期天晚上七点半。					

Notes 注解

The radical "女" is called "女字旁 [nǚzìpáng]". It is the changed form of "女 [nǚ] (female)". Sinograms with the radical "女" all have meanings related to "妇女 [fùnǚ] (women)".

字基(部首) "女" 是 "女" 字的变体，叫做 "女字旁"。凡是 "女(女字旁)" 的字都跟 "妇女" 的意思有关。

Vocabulary 词语

女 [nǚ]	female; daughter	女儿 [nǚ'ér]	daughter
妇 [fù]	woman; wife	妇科 [fùkē]	gynecology
奶 [nǎi]	milk; grandma	奶奶 [nǎinai]	grandma
姑 [gū]	(paternal) aunt	姑娘 [gūniang]	girl; young lady
姨 [yí]	(maternal) aunt	阿姨 [āyí]	aunt (address for a woman of one's parents' generation)
姐 [jiě]	elder sister	大姐 [dàjiě]	sister (address for a woman of one's generation)
妹 [mèi]	younger sister	姐妹 [jiěmèi]	sister
妙 [miào]	wonderful; clever	妙龄 [miàolíng]	youthfulness (of a girl)
娇 [jiāo]	delicate; pamper	娇养 [jiāoyǎng]	over-indulge
媒 [méi]	go-between	媒体 [méitǐ]	media
婚 [hūn]	marry; marriage	婚礼 [hūnlǐ]	wedding

I have a stomach ache.
我肚子疼。 Wǒ dùzi téng.

① Subjective 主体	② Possessing 领有	③ State 状态
you 你 [nǐ]		what symptoms 哪里不舒服 [nǎli bù shūfu]
I 我 [wǒ]		stomachache 肚子疼 [dùzi téng]
he 他 [tā]	have { 有 [yǒu]}	cough 咳嗽 [késou]
she 她 [tā]		headache 头痛 [tótòng]
my friend 我的朋友 [wǒ de péngyou]		fever 发烧 [fāshāo]
Sentence Making 造句 [zàojù]	What symptoms do you have? I have a fever.	你哪里不舒服? 我发烧了。

Notes 注解

The meaning of the radical "月" is not "月 [yuè] (moon)", but "肌肉 [jīròu] (muscle)". It is called "肌字旁 [jīzìpáng]". Sinograms with the radical "月" all have meanings related to 肌肉 or 内脏 [nèizàng](internal organs of the body).
字基(部首)"月"的意义不是"月亮",而是"肌肉",叫做"月(肌字旁)"。凡是有"月(肌字旁)"的字都跟"肌肉"或"内脏"的意思有关。

Vocabulary 词语

肌 [jī]	muscle	脏 [zàng]	viscera; internal organs
脸 [liǎo]	face	肝 [gān]	liver
肢 [zhī]	limb	肺 [fèi]	lung
脚 [jiǎo]	foot	脾 [pí]	spleen
肘 [zhǒu]	elbow	胆 [dǎn]	gall
股 [gǔ]	thigh	肠 [cháng]	intestine
胸 [xiōng]	chest	胃 [wèi]	stomach
腰 [yāo]	waist	肾 [shèn]	kidney
肚子 [dùzi]	abdomen; belly	肩 [jiān]	shoulder
脖子 [bózi]	neck	背 [bèi]	back

What disease is he suffering from?
他有什么病？ Tā yǒu shénme bìng?

He is suffering from heart disease.
他有心脏病。 Tā yǒu xīnzàngbìng.

	① Subjective 主体	② Undergoing 遭受	③ Objective 主体
	he 他 [tā]	suffer from 有 [yǒu]	what disease 什么病 [shénme bìng]
	your friend 你的朋友 [nǐ de péngyou]		heart disease 心脏病 [xīnzàngbìng]
			lung disease 肺病 [fèibìng]
	Wang Lin 王林 [Wáng Lín]		stomach disease 胃病 [wèibìng]
Sentence Making 造句 [zàojù]	What disease is your friend suffering from? My friend is suffering from stomach disease.	你的朋友有什么病？ 我的朋友有胃病。	

Vocabulary 词语

感冒 [gǎnmào]	flu; have a cold	流行病 [liúxíngbìng]	epidemic disease
贫血 [pínxuè]	anemia	慢性病 [mànxìngbìng]	chronic disease
霍乱 [huòluàn]	cholera	白血病 [báixuèbìng]	leukemia
痢疾 [lìji]	dysentery	冠心病 [guànxīnbìng]	coronary heart disease
疟疾 [nüèji]	malaria	结核病 [jiéhébìng]	tuberculosis
天花 [tiānhuā]	smallpox	糖尿病 [tángniàobìng]	diabetes
白喉 [báihóu]	diphtheria	艾滋病 [àizībìng]	AIDS
湿疹 [shīzhěn]	rash	结肠癌 [jiécháng' ái]	colon cancer
水痘 [shuǐdòu]	varicella; chickenpox	乳腺癌 [rǔxiàn' ái]	breast cancer
疥疮 [jièchuāng]	scabies	食管癌 [shíguǎn' ái]	esophageal cancer
黄疸 [huángdǎn]	jaundice	大脑炎 [dànǎoyán]	encephalitis
肿瘤 [zhǒngliú]	tumor	关节炎 [guānjiéyán]	arthritis
肺炎 [fèiyán]	pneumonia	气管炎 [qìguǎnyán]	tracheitis
肝炎 [gānyán]	hepatitis	中耳炎 [zhōng' ěryán]	otitis media
肠炎 [chángyán]	enteritis	脑膜炎 [nǎomóyán]	meningitis
咽炎 [yānyán]	pharyngitis	阑尾炎 [lánwěiyán]	appendicitis

What departments are there in this hospital?

这个医院有哪些科室？ Zhège yīyuàn yǒu nǎxiē kēshì?

There is a surgical department in this hospital.

这个医院有外科。 Zhège yīyuàn yǒu wàikē.

① Location 地点		② Existing 存在	③ Subjective 主体
Determiner 限定	Place 处所		
this 这个 [zhège]			what department 哪些科室 [nǎxiē kēshì]
	hospital 医院 [yīyuàn]	there be 有 [yǒu]	surgical department 外科 [wàikē]
			department of internal medicine 内科 [nèikē]
which 哪个 [nǎge]			department of orthopedic 骨科 [gǔkē]
Sentence Making 造句 [zàojù]	What departments are there in this hospital? There is a department of orthopedics in this hospital.		这个医院有哪些科室？ 这个医院有骨科。

Vocabulary 词语

外科 [wàikē]	surgical department	挂号处 [guàhàochù]	registration office
内科 [nèikē]	internal medicine	候诊室 [hòuzhěnshì]	waiting room
牙科 [yákē]	dental department	急诊室 [jízhěnshì]	emergency room
眼科 [yǎnkē]	ophthalmology	手术室 [shǒushùshì]	operating room
产科 [chǎnkē]	obstetrics	化验室 [huàyànshì]	laboratory
妇科 [fùkē]	gynecology	消毒室 [xiāodúshì]	disinfecting room
骨科 [gǔkē]	orthopedics	注射室 [zhùshèshì]	injecting room
小儿科 [xiǎo' érkē]	pediatrics	电疗室 [diànliáoshì]	electrotherapy room
神经科 [shénjīngkē]	neurology	透视室 [tòushìshì]	X-ray room
皮肤科 [pífūkē]	dermatology	病历室 [bìnglìshì]	medical record room
泌尿科 [mìniàokē]	urology	交费处 [jiāofèichù]	payment office
放射科 [fàngshèkē]	radiology	取药处 [qǔyàochù]	pharmacy

What symptoms of the patient did the nurse check?
护士检查了病人的哪些方面？ Hùshi jiǎnchále bìngrén de nǎxiē fāngmiàn?

The nurse checked the patient's temperature.
护士量了病人的体温。 Hùshi liángle bìngrén de tǐwēn.

① Subjective 主体	② Verbal 述谓		③ Objective 客体	
	Action 行动	Postpositive 后助词	Determiner 限定	Substance 实体
	check 检查 [jiǎnchá]		patient's/of the patient 病人的 [bìngrén de]	what symptoms 哪些方面 [nǎxiē fāngmiàn]
nurse 护士 [hùshi]		{ } 了 [le]	my 我的 [wǒ de]	body temperature 体温 [tǐwēn] weight 体重 [tǐzhòng]
	take 量 [liáng]		his 他的 [tā de]	blood pressure 血压 [xuèyā]
Sentence Making 造句 [zàojù]	What symptoms of the patient did the nurse check? The nurse checked his blood pressure.		护士检查了病人的哪些方面？ 护士量了他的血压。	

Vocabulary 词语

护士 [hùshi]	nurse	量体温 [liáng tǐwēn]	take body temperature
护士长 [hùshizhǎng]	head nurse	量体重 [liáng tǐzhòng]	check weight
护理人员 [hùlǐ rényuán]	nursing staff	量血压 [liáng xuèyā]	take blood pressure
住院医师 [zhùyuànyīshī]	resident physician	输液 [shūyè]	transfusion
按摩师 [ànmóshī]	massager	验血 [yàn xuè]	blood test
营养师 [yíngyǎngshī]	nutritionist	验尿 [yàn niào]	urine test
药剂师 [yàojìshī]	druggist/pharmacist	验大便 [yàn dàbiàn]	feces test
麻醉师 [mázuìshī]	anaesthetist	打针 [dǎzhēn]	take/give an injection
化验员 [huàyànyuán]	laboratory technician	监护 [jiānhù]	observe
检验员 [jiǎnyànyuán]	checker	透视 [tòushì]	have an X-ray
监护员 [jiānhùyuán]	monitor	抢救 [qiǎngjiù]	emergency treatmert

What medicine did the doctor prescribe for the patient?

医生给病人开了什么药？ Yīshēng gěi bìngrén kāile shénme yào?

The doctor prescribed traditional Chinese medicine for the patient.

医生给病人开了中药。 Yīshēng gěi bìngrén kāile zhōngyào.

① Subjective 主体	② Beneficiary 涉体		③ Verbal 述谓		④ Objective 客体
	Prepositive 前辅词	Person 人	Action 行动	Postpositive 后助词	
		patient 病人 [bìngrén]			what medicine 什么药 [shénme yào]
doctor 医生 [yīshēng]	for 给 [gěi]	you 你 [nǐ]	prescribe 开 [kāi]	{ } 了 [le]	traditional Chinese medicine 中药 [zhōngyào]
		me 我 [wǒ]			western medicine 西药 [xīyào]
		her 她 [tā]			penicillin 青霉素 [qīngméisù]

Sentence Making 造句 [zàojù]
What medicine did the doctor prescribe for you? 医生给你开了什么药？
The doctor prescribed penicillin for me. 医生给我开了青霉素。

Vocabulary 词语

外科医生 [wàikē yīshēng]	surgeon	西药 [xīyào]	western medicine
内科医生 [nèikē yīshēng]	physician	草药 [cǎoyào]	herbal medicine
牙科医生 [yákē yīshēng]	dentist	特效药 [tèxiàoyào]	specific medicine
妇科医生 [fùkē yīshēng]	gynecologist	解毒药 [jiědúyào]	antidote
产科医生 [chǎnkē yīshēng]	obstetrician	止血药 [zhǐxuèyào]	hemostatic
产科女医生 [chǎnkē nǚyīshēng]	accoucheuse	止泻药 [zhǐxièyào]	antidiarrheal
眼科医生 [yǎnkē yīshēng]	oculist	消炎药 [xiāoyányào]	antiphlogistic
耳科医生 [ěrkē yīshēng]	otologist	青霉素 [qīngméisù]	penicillin
儿科医生 [érkē yīshēng]	pediatrician	链霉素 [liànméisù]	streptomycin
皮肤科医生 [pífūkē yīshēng]	dermatologist	金霉素 [jīnméisù]	aureomycin
神经科医生 [shénjīngkē yīshēng]	neurologist	氯霉素 [lǜméisù]	chloromycetin
理疗科医生 [lǐliáokē yīshēng]	physiatrist	土霉素 [tǔméisù]	oxytetracycline
放射科医生 [fàngshèkē yīshēng]	radiologist	维生素 [wéishēngsù]	vitamin

责任编辑：贾寅淮　陆　瑜
英文编辑：郭　辉　薛彧威　范逊敏
封面设计：Jason Hao
印刷监制：佟汉冬

图书在版编目（CIP）数据

100句式汉语通：汉英对照 / 鲁川,孙文访著. —北京：华语教学出版
社，2011
　ISBN 978-7-5138-0036-5

　Ⅰ.①100… Ⅱ.①鲁… ②孙… Ⅲ.①汉语－句法－对外汉语教学－
教学参考资料 Ⅳ.①H195.4

　中国版本图书馆 CIP 数据核字（2011）第 033048 号

100句式汉语通

鲁　川　孙文访 著

*

©华语教学出版社
华语教学出版社出版
（中国北京百万庄大街24号　邮政编码 100037）
电话：（86）10-68320585 68997826
传真：（86）10-68997826 68326333
网址: www.sinolingua.com.cn
电子信箱: hyjx@sinolingua.com.cn
北京密兴印刷有限公司印刷
2011 年（16开）第 1 版
2011 年第 1 次印刷
（汉英）
ISBN 978-7-5138-0036-5
定价: 49.00 元